EGYPT

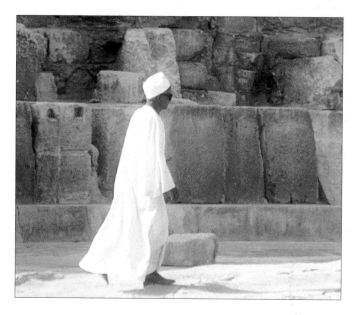

BY

MICHAEL HAAG

Produced by

Thomas Cook Publishing

Written by Michael Haag

Original photography by Rick Strange

Edited and designed by Laburnum
Technologies Pvt Ltd, C-533 Triveni Apts,
Sheikh Sarai Phase 1, New Delhi 110017

Published by Thomas Cook Publishing
A division of Thomas Cook Holdings Ltd

PO Box 227, The Thomas Cook Business
Park, Units 19–21, Coningsby Road,
Peterborough PE3 8XX, United Kingdom
E-mail: books@thomascook.com
www.thomascookpublishing.com

ISBN: 1-841572-50-0

Text © 2002 Thomas Cook Publishing
Maps © 2002 Thomas Cook Publishing
First edition © 2002 Thomas Cook Publishing

Managing Director: Kevin Fitzgerald

Publisher: Donald Greig

Series Consultant: Vivien Stone

All rights reserved. No part of this publication may be reproduced,
stored in a retrieval system or transmitted, in any form or by any means,
electronic, mechanical, recording or otherwise, in any part of the world,
without prior permission of the publisher. Requests for permission
should be addressed to Thomas Cook Publishing, PO Box 227,
The Thomas Cook Business Park, Units 19–21, Coningsby Road,
Peterborough, PE3 8XX, United Kingdom.

Although every care has been taken in compiling this publication, and
the contents are believed to be correct at the time of printing, Thomas
Cook Holdings Ltd cannot accept any responsibility for errors or
omissions, however caused, or for changes in details given in the
guidebook, or for the consequences of any reliance on the information
provided.

The opinions and assessments expressed in this book do not necessarily
represent those of Thomas Cook Holdings Ltd.

Printed and bound in Spain by: Grafo Industrias Gráficas, Basauri

Cover: Statue of Ramses II at Luxor Temple. Photograph by Rick
Strange.
Inside cover: photographs supplied by Spectrum Colour Library

CD manufacturing services provided by business interactive ltd,
Rutland, UK

Contents

Introduction

Pervaded with an impressive sense of permanence and duration, Egypt is an eternal amalgam of two elements: the constancy of the Nile, and the labours of its people. Five thousand years of history have been fashioned from these givens. Like the gigantic bird migrations that sweep up the valley, storming foreigners (Persian, Greek, Arab, Turkish, British) have passed across Egypt in magnificent spectacle, but in their wake the country has remained essentially unchanged. Egyptians are warm, friendly and generous, ambitious, intelligent, religious, and proud. Above all, they are open, and sometimes so insistent that the first-time visitor is likely to be confused, his reactions and emotions swinging like a pendulum. Yet, if you can take the pace, the sheer vitality of the Egyptian people becomes a wonderful roller-coaster ride, guaranteed to brighten your visit.

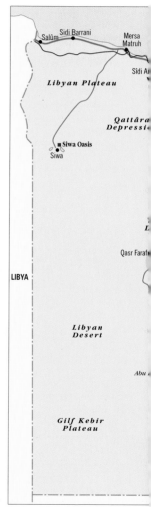

'*About Egypt I shall have a great deal more to relate because of the number of remarkable things which the country contains, and because of the fact that more monuments which beggar description are to be found there than anywhere in the world.*'

HERODOTUS

The Histories, c.430 BC

Land and People

Covering a total area of 1,002,000sq km, Egypt occupies the extreme northeast corner of the African continent, and the Sinai peninsula, which is in Asia. It is bounded to the west by Libya, to the south by Sudan, to the east by the Red Sea and Israel, and to the north by the Mediterranean.

Desert meets rock in Sinai

Central and southern Sinai is mountainous, its peaks ranging from 750m to 1,500m, though Gebel Musa (Mount Sinai) rises to 2,285m, and the summit of Gebel Katarina, the highest mountain in Egypt, is 2,642m. The mountain range running down the mainland's Red Sea coast is between 350m and 750m high. Otherwise, Egypt is a low, flat country, the Western Desert averaging 200m above sea level, while the Nile falls only 87m in its journey of some 1,000km northwards from Aswân to the Mediterranean sea. North of Cairo the river divides in two, its arms passing through the Delta and debouching into the sea at Rashid (Rosetta) and Dumyât (Damietta).

About 10,000 years ago a dramatic change in climate caused the once fertile lands of northern Africa and the Middle East to turn to dust, and their people migrated to the few remaining riverine areas. The Nile provided water, and its annual flood covered the valley with rich alluvial soil. But the river had to be regulated, swamps drained, canals dug, fields planted and irrigated – an entire complex system maintained. To this task Egypt's peasants, the *fellahin*, gave their labour, and the state provided direction.

Upper and Lower Egypt

Though it sometimes confuses the modern traveller to find Upper Egypt at the bottom of the map and Lower Egypt at the top, Memphis, the ancient capital just south of present-day Cairo, was deliberately sited to exercise a united authority over the upriver valley land (Upper Egypt), and the downriver Delta land (Lower Egypt).

The ancient Egyptians felicitously likened their united land to a lotus plant. The river valley was the stem, the Faiyûm the bud, the Delta the flower. Yet this slender figure of fertility covers less than 10 per cent of modern Egypt's total area, and within it lives 95 per cent of the nation's population, its density one of the highest in the world. The rest of the country is desert, where only a few Bedouin and oasis-dwellers can survive.

Apart from its Mediterranean coastline, where Alexandria enjoys an annual rainfall of 184mm, Egypt is exceptionally arid. Cairo receives only 24mm of rain a year, while the rest of the country receives less than even 10mm. Without the Nile, aptly known as the River of Life, there could be no agriculture in Egypt.

The Nile

Until the completion of the High Dam at Aswân in 1971, all life in Egypt depended on the annual rise and fall of the Nile. The river fell throughout the winter months, reaching its lowest level in May. In June it began to rise again, reaching its peak in September. The rising Nile, which came at precisely the driest and hottest time in the Egyptian year, was caused by spring and summer rains in the African interior. The inundation also brought with it millions of tons of mineral-rich sediment.

The Nile has now backed up behind the High Dam to create Lake Nasser.

Capable of holding several times more water than Egypt's annual requirement, the lake ensures a steady year-round flow from one year to the next, and so protects the country from Africa's droughts and famines.

There are ecological drawbacks, however, including the dependence on artificial fertilisers instead of silt. Also, the ancient land of Nubia, which stretched from the First Cataract at Aswân south into Sudan, has vanished beneath the lake. Most of the displaced Nubians, a distinct ethnic group, have been resettled around Kom Ombo, to the north of the dam.

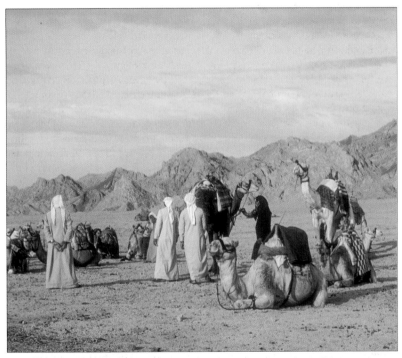

Bedouins and their camels stop for a much needed break while traversing the Sinai desert

History

As you will discover when visiting a museum or a site, or when reading almost anything about ancient Egypt, it is the usual practice to date pharaohs, monuments and artefacts in terms of dynasties rather than by years. The system began with the ancient priests and has been adopted by Egyptologists. Additionally, Egyptologists – though not the ancient Egyptians themselves – have grouped the various dynasties into broader periods, for example, Old Kingdom and New Kingdom.

Relief carving at Tell el Amarna's rock tombs

The Royal Dynasties of Ancient Egypt

Priests traditionally recorded long lists of Egypt's monarchs, describing the key events of individual pharaoh's reigns. Most Egyptologists are in agreement that these recordings were done in stone, although some say that lists also exist in papyrus (one of them being in Italy). An example is the list of Seti I's predecessors at Abydos (see p84).

Working from such lists, Manetho, an Egyptian priest under the early Ptolemies, arranged all the rulers of Egypt from Menes to Alexander into 31 dynasties. His lists can be seen at the Karnak Temple in Luxor, and also in a tomb at Saqqâra.

Egyptologists have relied on Manetho's list and have been able to confirm its essential correctness while sometimes improving upon it. The dates they have attached to the dynasties, however, are subject to varying margins of error, up to 100 years for the third millenium BC, around 10 years from 2000 BC onwards. Periods, dynasties, and their dates are listed below, along with some of the more important pharaohs and events associated with them.

First Dynastic Period 3100–2700 BC

1st Dynasty	3100–2800 BC Menes (Narmer) unites Upper and Lower Egypt; establishes Memphis as his capital.
2nd Dynasty	2800–2700 BC

Old Kingdom 2700–2200 BC
Period of stability.

3rd Dynasty	2700–2650 BC Zoser builds the Step Pyramid at Saqqâra.
4th Dynasty	2650–2500 BC Chephren, Cheops, and Mycerinus build their pyramids at Gîza.

5th **Dynasty**	2500–2350 BC Saqqâra pyramid built.

6th **Dynasty**	2350–2200 BC

First Intermediate Period
2200–2000 BC
Collapse of central authority.

7th & 8th **Dynasties**	2180–2155 BC

9th & 10th **Dynasties**	2155–2055 BC

11th **Dynasty**	2055–2000 BC

Middle Kingdom 2000–1800 BC
Egypt reunited. Conquest of Nubia.

12th **Dynasty**	2000–1780 BC Major building works and hydrological programmes in the Faiyûm.

Second Intermediate Period
1800–1550 BC
Collapse of central authority.

13th–17th **Dynasties**	1780–1570 BC The alien Hyksos people rule in Lower Egypt from 1730–1570 BC. The chariot is introduced.

New Kingdom 1570–1090 BC
Period of power, luxury and cosmopolitanism.

18th **Dynasty**	1570–1305 BC Hyksos expelled; royal residence, political and religious capital at Thebes. Grandiose building works at Thebes and Karnak. *Tuthmosis I*, 1525–1495 BC, initiates burials in Valley of the Kings. *Hatshepsut*, 1486–1468 BC, is regent for, then co-ruler with, Tuthmosis III, whom she over-shadows in her lifetime. Builds magnificent mortuary temple in Theban necropolis. *Tuthmosis III*, 1490–1436 BC, a great military leader, lays foundation for African and Asian empire. *Amenophis III*, 1398–1361 BC. Apogee of New Kingdom opulence. *Amenophis IV* (Akhenaton), 1369–1353 BC, opposes priesthood of Amun; moves capital to Tell el Amarna; establishes worship of the Aton. His queen is Nefertiti. *Tutankhamun*, 1352–1344 BC. Return to the worship of Amun.

19th **Dynasty**	1305–1200 BC *Seti I*, 1302–1290 BC, revives Old Kingdom style. *Ramses II*, 1290–1224 BC. Prodigious builder, for example, the Ramesseum and Abu Simbel.

20th Dynasty — 1200–1090 BC
Egypt enters the Iron Age. *Ramses III*, 1195–1164 BC, defeats Sea Peoples; he is the last great pharaoh.

Late Dynastic Period
1090–332 BC
Period of decline; often foreign rule.

21st Dynasty — 1090–945 BC
Capital at Tanis.

22nd Dynasty — 945–745 BC
Libyan origin.

23rd Dynasty — 745–718 BC
Ethiopian kings control Upper Egypt.

24th Dynasty — 718–712 BC. Ethiopian kings control the whole of Egypt.

25th Dynasty — 712–663 BC
Taharka, an Ethiopian king, builds First Pylon at Karnak; defeated by Assyrians; sack of Thebes.

26th Dynasty — 663–525 BC
Delta rulers, their capital at Sais; Assyrians ejected with Greek help. *Necho*, 610–595 BC, attempts to link Red Sea and Mediterranean by canal. Circumnavigation of Africa.

27th Dynasty — 525–404 BC
Persian rule.

28th Dynasty — 404–399 BC
Persians ejected with Greek help.

29th Dynasty — 399–380 BC
Delta remains centre of power.

30th Dynasty — 380–343 BC
Nectanebos I, 380–343 BC, builds at Philae.

31st Dynasty — 343–332 BC
Persian rule. Alexander the Great makes Egypt part of his empire in 332 BC.

323–282 BC — *Ptolemy I Soter*, one of Alexander's generals, makes himself king of Egypt and establishes the Ptolemaic dynasty that rules the country to the death of Cleopatra in 30 BC. He founds the Mouseion with its Library at Alexandria, which, like the Ptolemies themselves, is Greek in culture. Upriver, the Ptolemies preserve the old-style pharaonic architecture and religion.

282–246 BC — *Ptolemy II Philadelphos* builds the Pharos in Alexandria.

246–221 BC — *Ptolemy III Euergetes* builds at Karnak; begins temple of Edfu.

221–205 BC	*Ptolemy IV Philopator* begins temples at Esna and Kom Ombo.
80–51 BC	*Ptolemy XII Neos Dionysos* staves off Roman annexation. Builds at Dendera, Edfu and Philae.
51–30 BC	*Cleopatra VII.* Her policy is to preserve Egyptian power by joining forces with Rome. Through Julius Caesar, and then Mark Antony, she nearly succeeds.
30 BC	Octavian (later Augustus Caesar) captures Alexandria. Cleopatra and Antony commit suicide; Egypt becomes a Roman province.
AD 45	According to legend, St Mark introduces Christianity to Egypt.
249–251	Reign of Decius; severe Christian persecutions.
251–356	Life of St Antony, the world's first hermit.
284–305	Reign of Diocletian. His accession marks the beginning of the 'Era of Martyrs', the persecutions from which the Copts date their calendar.
313	Edict of Milan, tolerating Christianity.
About 330	Founding of the world's first monasteries, at Wadi Natrûn.
379–395	Reign of Theodosius I. He declares Christianity the official religion of the Roman Empire, which is now partitioned. Egypt is ruled from Constantinople, capital of the East Roman (Byzantine) Empire.

Detail of painting in Serenput II's tomb

AD **451**	Council of Chalcedon declares the monophysite Egyptian (Coptic) Church heretical.
476	Fall of the Roman Empire in the West.
622	Mohammed's flight from Mecca, the *hegira*, from which the Muslim calendar is reckoned.
640	Arab invasion of Egypt. Babylon (Old Cairo) falls in 641; Alexandria surrenders in 642.
878	Ibn Tulun, Abbassid governor of Egypt, makes himself independent of the Abbassid caliphate at Baghdad.
969	Cairo founded by Fatimids who invade Egypt from North Africa.
971	El Azhar founded.
1099	Crusaders take Jerusalem.
1171	Saladin founds his Ayyubid dynasty in Egypt; fortifies the Citadel. He recaptures Jerusalem in 1187.
1250–1517	Egypt ruled by Mameluke sultans, whose great builders include Qalaun (1279–90), Hassan (1347–61), Qaytbay (1469–95), and El Ghuri (1500–16).
Early 1300s	Severe persecution of the Copts, still half the population of Egypt; mass conversions to Islam follow.
1517	Egypt becomes part of the Ottoman Empire.
1798–1801	French occupation.
1805–49	Mohammed Ali makes himself master of Egypt. Begins modernisation, refounds Alexandria, and establishes dynasty which lasts until Nasser's revolution.
1869	Opening of the Suez Canal.
1882	Nationalist uprising against Turkish and European influence. British occupy Egypt.
1936	Anglo-Egyptian Treaty, formally ending British occupation of Egypt, except for Canal Zone.

1939–45	British army re-enters Egypt to repel Italians and Germans. Rommel defeated at El Alamein in 1942.
1948	British leave Palestine; creation of state of Israel. Arab-Israeli war.
1952	Army officers led by Nasser stage coup; King Farouk abdicates.
1956	Nasser nationalises the Suez Canal; Israel, France and Britain invade Egypt, but withdraw after international protest.
1967	Israel attacks and defeats Egypt in the 'Six Day War', and occupies Sinai.
1970	Nasser dies; Sadat becomes president.
1971	Completion of the Aswân High Dam.
1973	October War; Egyptian army crosses the canal.
1977	Sadat visits Jerusalem in dramatic peace bid.
1981	Sadat assassinated by Muslim fundamentalists. Hosni Mubarak becomes president.

1982	Israel evacuates Sinai.
1984–98	Political and economic liberalisation, but also a rise in Islamic conservatism.
1998–	Economic stagnation due to external events and internal unrest. However, since 1999, there has been no Islamist militant activity of note.

Roman pillar at Babylon, Old Cairo

Governance

The United Arab Republic (UAR), to give Egypt its official title, has its capital at Cairo. Its chief executive is the president, who is elected for a six-year term. He determines the country's policies, is head of the armed forces, and he nominates the vice-president, the prime minister, and other high political, civil, and military officials.

THOMAS COOK'S
EGYPT

The People's Assembly, all but 10 of its 454 members elected by popular vote for a five-year term, is the legislative body, advised by the Consultative Assembly which functions only in an advisory capacity. The Constitution guarantees freedom of religion and thought, declares Islam to be the official religion of the state, and announces that the principles of Islamic law (*Sharia*) constitute the inspiring fount of legislation.

In the pyramid of the Egyptian state, however, the summit imposes itself on the base. There is freedom of the press, but it is undermined by sycophancy; elections take place under laws biased in favour of the ruling National Democratic Party.

Nasser's Legacy

The country is still burdened by Nasser's legacy. Whatever his nationalist ideals, he was a dictator whose socialist policies helped wreck the economy. Until recently, people were content to depend on subsidies. Before the deposition of King Farouk in 1952, education accounted for more than 12 per cent of government spending, and defence, under 10 per cent. Defence now eats 30 per cent, while education receives only six per cent. Pre-revolutionary Egypt was self-sufficient in food, and its foreign exchange reserves were US $25 billion in today's terms. Now it must import at least half its food, it has a national debt of around US $30 billion, and were it not for foreign aid – mainly from the US – the economy would collapse.

There have been some improvements. Today, nearly all households have

Egypt is the country most closely associated with the history of Thomas Cook. Cook was invited to the opening of the Suez Canal in 1869 and opened an office in Cairo. He was nearly drowned on his first Nile excursion, but survived to become owner of a fleet of 40 Nile cruisers. As the sole agent for mail and passenger traffic in Egypt, he was largely responsible for creating the booming tourist trade the country knows today. In 1884, when General Gordon was besieged by the Mahdi in Khartoum, Cook was asked to provide the transport for an Anglo-Egyptian force of 30,000 men and 100,000 tons of stores.

television and VCRs, where few had even electricity before the revolution. Diet has improved along with working conditions for many. Infant mortality has been sharply reduced, and literacy has doubled, although illiteracy is still high at 36 per cent. There are 60 times as many cars.

The yawning gap between rich and poor still remains. Under the monarchy the 2,000 richest people owned as much land as the 1.5 million poorest peasants. Today, 70,000 Egyptians own Mercedes cars, each one worth the lifetime salary of a factory worker.

Recent Developments

After the revolution in 1952, nearly a quarter of a million foreigners, most of them highly skilled, were forced to leave. In recent years three million Egyptians have followed in their footsteps, seeking opportunities in the Gulf and the West.

A real effort is being made to renovate the once-beautiful cities of Cairo and Alexandria, but stretches of the north and Red Sea coasts have fallen victim to unplanned growth. Attention is being paid to newer developments such as Sharm El Sheikh in order to avoid similiar mistakes.

The political failures since 1952 have blocked an effective response to Egypt's greatest problem – its rocketing birth rate. The population now stands at about 65 million, and increases by one million every nine months, outstripping land reclamation, food production, and the creation of new jobs. The need for birth control apart, the government has belatedly removed subsidies, by encouraging private enterprise, and increased productivity. Sudden reforms, however, could further impoverish the poor and cause massive job losses and political unrest. Anxiety and discontent have been exploited in the past by Islamic fundamentalists.

Yet, with ample resources of water and land, with oil, an ideal location for trade, a large and cheap workforce, private capital, unparalleled tourist attractions, and a high degree of social cohesion, the country also enjoys considerable advantages upon which to build a bright future.

Efforts at restoration are still to touch many parts of Cairo

Religion

Until the Arab invasion in AD 641, Egypt was a Christian country, but within 500 years the majority of Egyptians had become Muslims. About 10 per cent of the population, however, has remained Christian, and are called Copts, a corruption of the Greek word for Egypt, *Aigyptos*.

There are no physical differences between Copts and Muslims. Nor do they differ in language or culture. Both groups are proud to call themselves Egyptians, and live harmoniously together.

COPTIC CHURCH

Orthodox Coptic rituals include fasting and conducting the Mass with 30 per cent of the prayers still in the Coptic language. The Coptic *Deskilia* – a book of teachings said to have been handed down from St Mark to the Coptic Orthodox Church – is still used.

Christians

St Mark is the legendary 1st-century founder of Christianity in Egypt. From its earliest roots among the Jews and Greeks of Alexandria, Christianity soon spread among the native population, where it resonated with such ancient Egyptian notions as resurrection and the afterlife. Isis and the infant Horus, for example, resemble the Virgin and Child, and it was no accident that a native-born Egyptian theologian of Alexandria first pronounced Mary to be the Mother of God. Monasticism also began in Egypt and went on to make a profound spiritual impact on the world.

By the 5th century, the Roman and Byzantine empires had split, and Egypt was ruled from Constantinople. Soon a theological argument, abetted by nationalist undercurrents, developed. In Constantinople and Rome, it was held that Christ had two separate natures, the human and the divine. However, Alexandrian theologians, while admitting the two natures, emphasised their unity. For this they were called

monophysites (believers in only one nature), and were charged with heresy at the Ecumenical Council of Chalcedon in 451, resulting in their break from Rome.

Had national pride not got in the way, the theological differences might have been overcome. But at the moment of the Arab invasion, Egypt was in a state of mutiny against the Byzantine Empire whose forces could do nothing but abandon the country. Over the centuries the Coptic Church turned in upon itself, preserving ancient rituals while failing to develop. It is now, however, experiencing a renaissance and has a flourishing congregation, while, in a new ecumenical spirit, links are being forged with Christian churches worldwide.

Muslims

Of the two predominant Muslim sects, Sunni and Shia, Egypt's Muslims are Sunnis. Unlike the Shias who claimed that the Prophet's successor, the next Caliph, be appointed by virtue of heredity, the Sunnis advocated succession by democratic consensus.

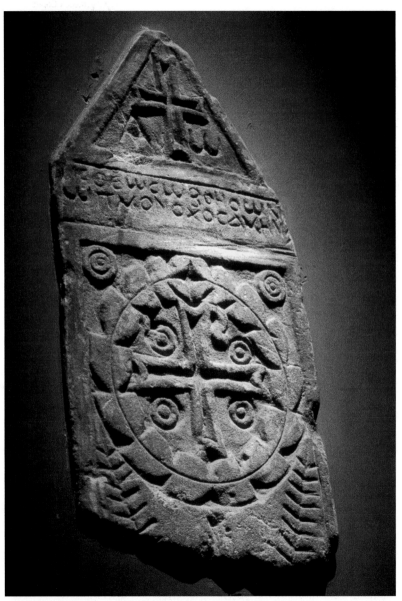

Relief carving with Christian motif, Museum of Antiquities, Luxor

Islam

The principal belief of Islam is the existence of one God, the same God worshipped by Jews and Christians, known to all Arabs as Allah. Islam means submission. Muslim means one who submits to one God as interpreted by the Prophet Mohammed.

Mohammed was a merchant in Arabia. He often went to contemplate in the desert, and at the age of 40 he had a vision of the angel Gabriel who commanded him to proclaim monotheism to the pagan Arabian tribes. He did so, and the words of Allah as given to Mohammed became known as the Quran. Concerned by the unsettling effects of this new religion, the merchants of Mecca drove Mohammed out of the city in 622. His flight (the *hegira*) from Mecca to Medina, where Islam first took root, marks the start of the Islamic calendar.

In Islam, the one who believes and worships approaches God directly and simply. All Muslims must perform five practical devotions, the five Pillars of Faith. They must pronounce the fundamental creed: 'I bear witness that there is no god but Allah and Mohammed is his prophet'; pray five times a day; give part of their income to charity; fast during Ramadan; and make the pilgrimage (Haj) to Mecca.

The most visible of these devotions is prayer. A muezzin makes the call to prayer, usually by loudspeaker these days, from the minaret of a mosque. Prayer may take place in a mosque, at home, at the office or anywhere, but worshippers always prostrate themselves in the direction of Mecca.

Westerners will be struck by the extent to which Islam permeates all areas of public and private life. This follows from the Quran, which is as much a book of laws and rules of conduct to be observed in day to day living, as it is a spiritual guide. Indeed, within Islam, there is no separation of the secular and religious life.

Facing page: The entrance of the El Hussein mosque, Cairo
Above: Typical Islamic mosque decoration
Below: A minaret of the mosque of Sultan Barquq, Cairo

Culture

Egyptian culture is Arabic, with something of an African feel. In Alexandria especially, and to a lesser extent in Cairo, there is additionally an atmosphere of the French, and of the Levant, with its amalgam of Greek, Turkish, and Syrian cultures. Cairo itself is distinctly cosmopolitan.

The desert is integral to the life of all Egyptians

Following the 7th-century AD Arab invasion, the new holders of power and patrons of culture spread the Arabic language and Islam which, with its prohibition on the depiction of human images, had a decisive effect in separating the greater part of Egypt's population from its pharaonic and Graeco-Roman past. The ancient inheritance only

A wandering Nubian musician

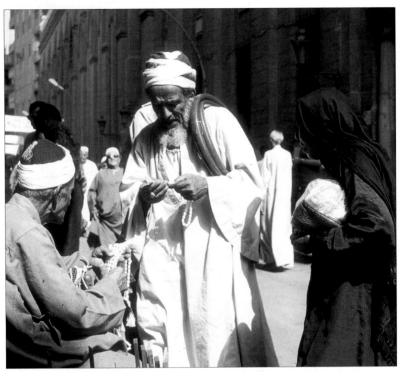

Bartering is a way of life on the streets of the city

survives in a much transmuted form within the Coptic Church (*see p16*).

The outlook and lifestyle of Egypt's urban middle class is not dissimilar to that of people living in Europe and America. In Cairo, for example, with its many bookshops, cafés and cinemas, its Opera House, its cultural societies and universities, there is ample opportunity to share in and contribute to the broad international experience.

Life is a grind for the poor in the cities, though many willingly seek the slender promise of a better life here rather than endure the monotonous labour of the countryside, largely unchanged since pharaonic times. Relief is provided by television and the cinema, but also by such popular celebrations as *moulids*, the Egyptian equivalent of medieval saints' anniversaries and fairs. Here, booths sell crafts and sweets, and marriages are arranged. There is music, the hypnotic whirling of dervishes, puppet shows, story-tellers, and dancing.

The novels of Naguib Mahfouz, who won the Nobel Prize in 1989, offer a vivid portrait of modern Egypt's multi-faceted society.

Festivals

Religious festivals, both Muslim and Christian, are often times of joyful public celebration. There is usually an atmosphere of infectious hospitality and bonhomie, and sometimes there is entertainment in the form of music and dancing, as well as special souqs. Almost all Muslim festivals are fixed in accordance with the 12 lunar months of the Islamic calendar, which means that they do not occur on the same date each year. (*See* National Holidays, *p185.*)

ISLAMIC MONTHS

Moharram
  1st month (30 days)
Safar
  2nd month (29 days)
Rabei el Awal
  3rd month (30 days)
Rabei el Tani
  4th month (29 days)
Gamad el Awal
  5th month (30 days)
Gamad el Tani
  6th month (29 days)
Ragab
  7th month (30 days)
Shaaban
  8th month (29 days)
Ramadan
  9th month (30 days)
Shawal
  10th month (29 days)
Zoul Qidah
  11th month (30 days)
Zoul Hagga
  12th month (29 days,
  30 in leap years)

Ramadan

During this month of fasting, practised by all good Muslims, nothing is permitted to pass the lips between sunrise and sunset. As it happens, more food is consumed in Egypt during Ramadan than in any other month of the year, everyone more than making up at night for what they gave up during the day. The nights, therefore, take on something of a carnival atmosphere. This can be a good time to stroll the streets, which are lit by coloured lanterns, and thronged with animated crowds, often with singing and dancing in the squares and cafés. In Cairo it is especially worth going to the square in front of the Sayyidna Hussein Mosque in Khan el Khalili.

At Luxor the festivities take place on the grass in front of the Mosque of Abu el Haggag at Luxor Temple.

Eid el Fitr

This three-day feast comes as a celebratory climax to Ramadan which it immediately follows. It is a time when families and friends come together.

Eid el Adha (Quarban Bairam)

This Great Feast, which celebrates Abraham's willingness to sacrifice Isaac, occurs from the 10th to the 13th of Zoul Hagga – the month when the Haj, or annual Pilgrimage, takes place. Everyone who can afford to, slaughters a sheep, and distributes a portion of it for the occasion.

Ras el Sana el Hegira

The Islamic New Year begins on the first day of the month of Moharram. Quranic and other religious texts are read at this time.

Muslim and Christian Moulids

A *moulid* is a festival in honour of a holy man, and its devotional aspects aside, it usually takes on the character of a medieval fair with popular entertainments and a souq.

The **Moulid el Nabi**, which is a nationwide Muslim celebration of the Prophet's birthday on the 12th day of Rabei el Awal, is marked in Cairo by a spectacular procession. The place to be is the square in front of the Sayyidna Hussein Mosque in Khan el Khalili.

Most *moulids*, however, are local affairs, albeit sometimes on a gigantic scale as at Tanta (*see p61*). The Moulid of Abu el Haggag, whose mosque sits atop the walls of Luxor Temple, occurs on the 14th of Shaaban, and is one of the largest and wildest in Upper Egypt. During the week leading up to St Shenute's *moulid* on 14 July, thousands of people from all over Upper Egypt attend the sprawling encampment of tented stalls at the White Monastery outside Sohâg, where the night is filled with drifting laughter, the aroma of cooked foods, and the sinuous sound of Egyptian music.

Whirling Dervishes

Mevlana, the 13th-century Sufi master who founded his sect of Whirling Dervishes at Konya in Turkey, has his followers in Egypt. Suspect, and indeed often banned in other Muslim countries, their intention is to achieve mystical union with God through ecstatic whirling. On Wednesdays and Saturdays from 8pm to 9pm, they can be seen at the cultural centre inside the El Ghuri Mausoleum on Sharia Muizz, Cairo.

Sham el Nessim

This national holiday, with its roots in the Christian and pharaonic traditions, falls on the first Monday after Coptic Easter. All Egyptians, of whatever religion, take the day off to celebrate the advent of spring, usually by picnicking.

Dawn prayers in Cairo during the three-day feast of Eid el Fitr

Impressions

Arriving in Egypt is like entering a bazaar. Your senses are invaded by its colour, its noise, its smells, its animation. Movement is eager, heaving, seemingly chaotic. Everything is thrust at you. Well, Egypt is something of a bazaar, and it is up to you how much you want to respond to what is on offer. At first you may feel overwhelmed and uncertain, but you are free to experience it at a relaxed pace. Nobody will mind if you take your time in getting the measure of the place.

'It is not well to drink much wine, beer, or spirits in Egypt, but coffee may be far more freely indulged in than in Europe or America. As regards smoking, most men come down to cigarettes or mild tobacco in native pipes.'
CHARLES G LELAND
The Egyptian Sketchbook, 1873

Arabic

The language of Egypt is Arabic. It is written from right to left, using an alphabet of 29 letters. There is no completely satisfactory system for conveying the sound of Arabic letters in Western languages. Nor is there agreement on the transliteration of Egyptian place-names. Therefore, Faiyûm might appear as Fayyum, Saqqâra as Sakkara, Dendera as Denderah, and so on. This can present an even bigger problem when the initial letters vary, for example, Edfu instead, of Idfu, or Qena instead of Kena. So do not rely entirely on spelling; instead, try to think phonetically when looking for places on maps, signs, and in this guide.

For the sake of simplicity, El (or el) has been used throughout this guide, for example, El Azhar is used rather than Al Azhar (or al-Azhar). The Arabic for street is *sharia*, and for square it is *midan* – at least those are the spellings that are used here. These come before the name, for example, Sharia Ramses, and Midan el Tahrir.

Inshallah, Bukra, and Maalesh

Part of Egyptian tradition, though increasingly out of date in today's faster-moving Egypt, are three commonly heard words, *inshallah, bukra,* and *maalesh*, whose meanings, and more importantly, whose nuances, you should know. Together they provide some insight into how things work, or frequently, do not work, in Egypt.

Inshallah means 'God willing', and, reasonably enough, it conveys the caution that even with the best of human intentions nothing can be certain, and everything is in the hands of Allah. However, it can also be a diplomatic way of saying that you cannot commit yourself, indeed, of even suggesting that the thing promised will not happen.

Bukra means 'tomorrow', but it would be a mistake to take this literally. *Bukra,* in fact, more usually refers to some indefinite point in time between tomorrow and never.

Maalesh can mean 'never mind', or 'it's alright'.

Baksheesh

The word *baksheesh* literally means 'share the wealth'. It is payable for all services, however small, and, as often as not, is expected for nothing at all. Alms-giving is a central tenet of Islam, and few Egyptians will balk at accepting their share. You have it, they do not, and so they feel you should pass it round.

Baksheesh is the tip you might give to the man who has carried your luggage. It is also the reward placed deftly in the outstretched hand of the guardian who lets you into a tomb after closing time, or given to the railway carriage attendant who discovers there is a sleeping compartment free after all. There may be times when you wish to give something out of charity – that, too, is *baksheesh*. But *baksheesh* can be a plague. Children may pester you for it in the streets, or you may have paid but are pressed for more.

The basic rule is to offer *baksheesh* only in return for a service, and not to pay until the service has been performed, and also to resist firmly any attempt at intimidation.

Passers-by may scent the tobaccco of the *nargileh* or *shisha*

Catching Cold

When you think of Egypt you think of sun and heat, and so you will, of course, think of taking light clothes, sunglasses, and a hat or scarf to protect yourself against sunstroke. But that is not the whole of the story. You need to be aware of the extremes of temperature in Egypt, and that can mean extremes of cold as well as heat. The desert can be punishingly hot by day, but it can rapidly become chilly, and outside the summer months, cold, as soon as the sun goes down. Even attending the Sound and Light show at the Gîza Pyramids on the edge of the desert can prove to be uncomfortably cool.

The same is true of the mountainous landscapes of Sinai and along the Red Sea coast – you could easily turn blue on top of Mount Sinai while waiting for the sun to rise. In the desert and the mountains you should carry a sweater with you at night, even in summer. *(For details of* Climate, *see pp177–8.)*

Living Standards

The living standards of a great number of Egyptians are very low, and visitors may be distressed at the poverty they will sometimes encounter. Egyptians, however, are a proud people. Family and neighbourhood networks serve as a form of social security system. There is little homelessness here. Numerous people may pack into a room, or families may live among the tombs in Cairo's City of the Dead, but no one sleeps out on the street. Outright begging is rare; the request for *baksheesh* usually supposes that some service has been performed. Your greatest contribution to the situation is to visit Egypt, for tourism creates jobs.

Manners and Customs

Egyptian values are rooted in the strong family attachments of a still over-whelmingly rural heritage, and in Islam's closely woven social code. Though allowances are made for foreign idiosyncrasies, and Egyptians have a more relaxed attitude to dress and behaviour, a degree of conservatism is expected from you. Physicality should be muted, so that men and women should refrain from kissing and hugging in public, while

SUPERSTITION

Superstition says that the envious glance of a passer-by, attracted by an immodest show of wealth, achievement, or beauty, can harm or bewitch. Reciting certain verses of the Quran is one way of warding it off; the Eye of Horus is another. It may be painted on cars, trucks, and fishing boats, or worn as an amulet, particularly by children, who are especially vulnerable to the 'evil eye'. Therefore, it is a good idea not to admire something too much – your behaviour can be mistaken for desire, and you may find that you are presented with the object of your attention.

generally, it is a good idea not to show too much flesh. Except at resorts such as Sharm El Sheikh and Hurghada, where pretty much anything goes, women should not wear shorts, dresses or skirts which are too short, and both women and men should cover their shoulders.

Do not photograph an Egyptian without asking permission. For some people it is extremely offensive, while others, who might not have minded, will feel that you have taken a liberty. If you do ask first, people are often happy to be photographed, and indeed, the occasion can be a way of getting to know people. Egyptians can be sensitive about many scenes you might find picturesque but which to them portray poverty or backwardness. If someone asks you to desist, it is best to do so and look for another chance elsewhere. Militarily sensitive subjects – including airports, railway stations, dams, bridges, and government offices – should definitely not be photographed.

During the month of Ramadan, Muslims may not eat, drink, or smoke while the sun is up. It would be polite if you, too, refrained, in public at least.

If you are invited to someone's home, it is customary to bring a gift, such as pastries or other local sweets.

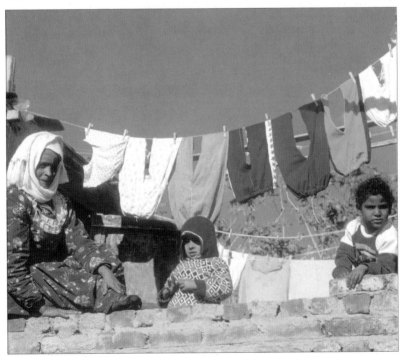

Make-shift home of a Bedouin family

The Arabic alphabet is completely different to that of other languages, but in general, street signs and all other notices relevant to the tourist will be written in English, or sometimes French. You may soon come to recognise one word, however, which you will frequently see not only in mosques, but on the walls of shops, restaurants, almost anywhere – the Arabic for Allah:

You should make an effort to learn the Arabic numerals (from which Western numerals have derived). This will help you identify numbered buses and railway carriages, and understand prices.

Hieroglyphs

Hieroglyphs began in around 3000 BC as picture writing, that is, the pictures

conveyed an idea or story. Soon a phonetic alphabet of 24 letters was introduced, and if only these had been used, then reading hieroglyphs would be easy. Additionally, however, the priests used more than 700 signs representing syllables. There are books available explaining how to read those symbols which are more common.

A distinctive feature of hieroglyphs is the cartouche, a stylised loop of rope which always encloses the name of a ruler, thereby conveying the idea of unending, unbroken, unchanging power. In the 1820s, Jean François Champollion guessed that cartouches enclosed the names of rulers. When he saw a number of cartouches on the Rosetta Stone, then saw repeated below these, in Greek, the names of several rulers, he was able to match Greek letters to hieroglyphic symbols (*see p126*).

K   L   I   O   P   A   D   R   A

Numerals

١	٢	٣	٤	٥	٦	٧	٨	٩	١٠
1	2	3	4	5	6	7	8	9	10

The Crown

Pharaohs are always shown wearing a crown, either the White Crown of Upper Egypt, or the Red Crown of Lower Egypt. The two are often combined to indicate the pharaoh's authority over a united Egypt. At the front of the crown is the *uraeus*, a hooded cobra, to ward off his enemies.

Right: Relief carving in the Temple of Hathor, Philae, showing the combined crown of Egypt illustrated above

Moustache

You do not actually need to have a moustache to be called one. 'Moustache', or more formally 'Mister Moustache', is what Egyptians, usually touts, sometimes call male foreigners. More generally, the foreigner, male or female, is called a *khawaga*, which also conveys the sense that you have lots of money which you are about to share (*see* Baksheesh, *p25*).

Security

Egypt is a safe country for visitors. You are far safer walking through the streets of Cairo, where muggings are unheard of, than through those of many European or American cities – and that is true both day and night.

There is a strong sense of communal responsibility, especially towards foreigners. Anyone in distress can expect the immediate assistance of both the public and the police.

In addition to the regular Metropolitan Police, who wear black uniforms in winter, white uniforms in summer, and who mostly speak only Arabic, there are special police who wear the same uniform but with a red armband saying 'Tourist Police'. They sometimes speak a foreign language, usually English (not necessarily fluently, however), and are posted at tourist sights, museums, airports, railway stations, and ports. They are there to help if you are experiencing difficulties.

There are also the more soldierly-looking Central Security Police, always in black and armed with automatic weapons, who guard embassies, banks, post offices, and other public buildings.

Egyptian police in summer uniform

A few fundamentalist fanatics who would like to turn Egypt into a theocratic Islamic state have attempted in the past to attack the government, and indeed the economy of the country, through tourism. By threatening and frightening away foreign visitors, their hope has been to destroy a major source of Egypt's income. Egyptians are, however, overwhelmingly opposed to such outrages, and the government has responded with determination, but, as in London or New York, it is never entirely possible to guarantee the elimination of terrorist activity. What can be said is that Egyptians remain a warm, good-humoured and hospitable people who care about the welfare of visitors to their country.

Touts

Touts are most common and relentless at the obvious tourist places, such as the Pyramids at Gîza, or along the corniche at Luxor. A polite but firm *la shukran* ('no thank you') should be enough to turn away unwanted attentions. If forced to rudeness, then *imshee* ('get lost') has the almost physical effect of a slap in the face. However, a kinder way to deter touts would be to say *sebne* ('leave me') or, if you can manage it, *sebne, lao samat* ('excuse me, leave me').

Do not assume that everyone is out to take advantage of you. People are often simply curious, or wish to be helpful.

Visiting Mosques and Monasteries

In visiting mosques and Christian monasteries, you are entering into the most conservative areas of Egyptian life, and therefore should take special care to dress and act with decorum. Shorts or short skirts should not be worn, nor should shoulders be bare. Inside mosques you must remove your shoes, or shoe coverings will be provided. For this, or if you accept the services of a guide, or ask to be shown the way up a minaret, *baksheesh* will be expected in addition to any entry fee.

You may sometimes find yourself in a mosque at prayer time. Then, although visitors are otherwise welcome, you may be asked to retreat into an alcove or out on to the street.

Except for St Catherine's Monastery in Sinai, which is Greek Orthodox, all Egyptian monasteries are Coptic. The Copts go in for a good deal of fasting, and during such periods their monasteries are closed to visitors. (*For further details*, see p178.)

Shoe rack outside a mosque – you must remove your footwear before entering

Women Travellers

Westerners going to Egypt are, to some extent, putting themselves in a position of contrast to the conventions of social life there, although in major tourist destinations a Western woman may never feel the cultural differences.

An Egyptian woman's life is very much bound up, indeed bounded, by her family relationships, whether as daughter, wife, or mother. The entwined moral, religious, and legal systems of the country enforce this. Even an educated woman would be most circumspect in her relationship with a man; both families would be involved, and meetings limited to public situations.

Your Western view may be that that is their business and your business is your own. Some Egyptians will make the effort to see it that way, especially as you are only passing through. A great many more will not agree.

Things are, however, changing in Egypt. In certain areas of Cairo and other cosmopolitan places, Egyptian women behave much like Westerners when it comes to dressing and having a good time. If in doubt in less tourist-exposed areas, dress conservatively.

A woman walking about or travelling on her own may be pestered but, as in other countries, it depends on how she chooses to dress and how she reacts. You can reduce the chances of being hassled by dressing and behaving conservatively. If it helps, wear a wedding ring. Or keep in the company of other women, for example, when travelling on a train. Egyptian women will happily adopt you into their circle.

There is no reason for you to put up with unwelcome attention. If, at worst, you are touched up, you can first say *imshee*, which means 'get lost'. If something stronger is called for, shout *sebne le wahadee*, which means 'leave me alone'. People will come to your aid, and the man will be so ashamed, he will probably run away.

Women mix freely with men in the market of Khan el Khalili

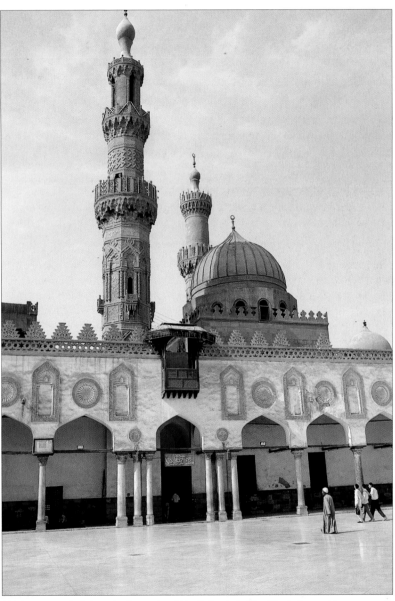

Al Azhar mosque in Cairo, a leading centre of Islamic theological teaching in the world

Cairo

Cairo is not only the largest city in Africa, but also the political and cultural pivot of the Arab world. Its population of around 15 million, swelling to 17 million on a daily basis, has grown five-fold within a generation, as *fellahin* (Egypt's peasantry) have poured in from the countryside in search of opportunities. New bridges, flyovers, and an excellent metro system keep the city from grinding to a halt, and there is constant new building.

The most modern part of the city lies close to the Nile, which breathes through Cairo like a giant lung. Further east, towards the Moqattam Hills, is the medieval city of splendid mosques and thronging bazaars, founded by the Fatimids in AD 969. To the south is the now ruinous Fustat, the earliest Arab settlement, built when the Arabs invaded Egypt around AD 641. Westwards, beyond the sprawl of Gîza, the Pyramids glow gold at sundown against the Western Desert as they have done for thousands of years.

'You can never in your thoughts detach the Egypt of the past from the Egypt of today; neither, indeed, can you ever quite exclude it from sight.'

HOWARD HOPLEY
Under Egyptian Palms, London, 1869

Abu Sarga Church (St Sargius)
See p47.
Old Cairo (Misr el Qadima). 4.5km south of Midan el Tahrir. Open: 8am–4pm. Free admission. Metro: Mari Girgis.

Aqueduct
Much of the 3.5km-long Mameluke aqueduct (AD 1505), which once brought water from the Nile to the Citadel, still survives. You can see it opposite the midpoint of Roda Island.

El Azhar Mosque
The El Azhar ('the most blooming') was completed in AD 971, the first mosque built by the Fatimids in their new city of Cairo. The world's foremost centre of Islamic theological teaching, it is also the oldest university in the world, with modern schools of medicine, science, and languages nearby.

Although much rebuilt in a confusion of styles, the overall impression is of harmony, the atmosphere venerable. Off the central court, theological teachers sit, surrounded by their students, as was done a thousand years ago. There are wonderful views of the medieval city from the roof and minarets.
Sharia el Azhar. 3km east of Midan el Tahrir. Open: winter, daily 9am–4pm; summer 9am–5pm. Closed: 11am–1pm during Friday prayers. Admission charge.

Central Cairo

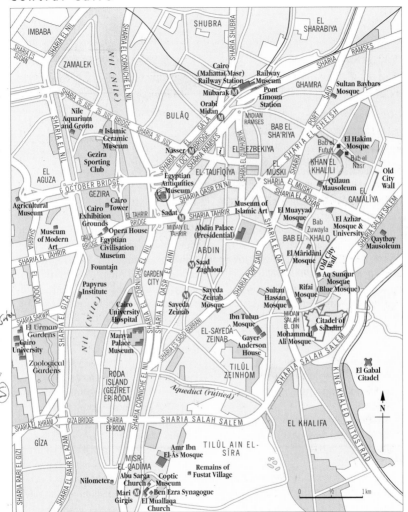

Bab Zuwayla, Bab el Futuh, and Bab el Nasr

The three surviving gates to the Fatimid city (*see p44*).

Nearby Khan el Khalili (*see p38 and p44*).

Bayt el Suhaymi

This merchant's house of the Ottoman period, built during the 16th and 17th centuries, and completely furnished from that time, is the finest house in Cairo, and a wonderful example of

The Citadel overlooks Midan Salah el Din, 3km southeast of Midan el Tahrir. Open: 9am–4pm. Closed: Friday 11.30am–1pm. Admission charge. The Carriage and Military Museums are extra.

Islamic secular architecture. Beautifully decorated rooms include the men's dining loggia, and the women's harem with its own private chapel and bathhouse, and bedrooms screened with intricately patterned *mashrabiyya* windows. Arranged around a garden courtyard, the dwelling is always deliciously cool.

Haret el Darb el Asfar, east of Sharia el Muizz. 3km east of Midan el Tahrir. Open: 9am–4pm. Admission charge.

Ben Ezra Synagogue
See p47.
Old Cairo (Misr el Qadima). Open: daily 9am–4pm. Free admission. Metro: Mari Girgis.

Cairo Tower
Rising like a giant lotus 187m above the island of Gezira, the tower's open observation platform and enclosed café and restaurant offer spectacular, panoramic views of the city.

Sharia el Burg el Qahira, towards the southern end of Gezira Island. 1km west of Midan el Tahrir. Open: 9am–midnight. Admission charge.

The Citadel
In 1176 Salah al-Din built his fortress on this spur of the Moqattam Hills, which commands a clear view of the whole of Cairo. For almost 700 years, to the death of Mohammed Ali in 1849, nearly all Egypt's rulers lived in the Citadel, held court, dispensed justice, and received ambassadors (*see p43*).

Bijou Palace
Mohammed Ali's palace, with its French-style salons, is now a museum of 19th-century royal portraits, sumptuous costumes and furnishings.

Citadel Museums
See p39.

El Nasr Mohammed Mosque
Built during the early 14th century by the Mameluke Sultan el Nasr Mohammed, the marble panelling and much of the faïence decoration of the exterior were long ago stripped away, creating an austere impression. The arcades around the central courtyard, however, remain elegant in their proportions, their columns taken from

ancient pharaonic, Roman, and Byzantine buildings.

Mohammed Ali Mosque

A Turkish delight on the Cairo skyline, the mosque was built in imitation of the Ottoman imperial mosques of Istanbul. Half domes rise as buttresses for the high central dome, while two thin minarets add an ethereal touch. Mohammed Ali's tomb is on the right as you enter the vast and opulently decorated interior. From the courtyard outside, pollution permitting, there is a superb view of the city.

Gayer-Anderson House

Named after a British major who restored and occupied what is in fact two 17th-century houses knocked together, the house is filled with his eclectic collection of English, French, and oriental furniture, and bric-à-brac which gives the place a lived-in feel. The large reception room is overlooked by a balcony enclosed by a *mashrabiyya* screen through which the women of the harem could discreetly observe male visitors.

Abuts the Ibn Tulun Mosque off Sharia el Salibah, 500m west of the Citadel. 3km southeast of Midan el Tahrir. Tel: 3647822. Open: 9am–4pm. Closed: Fri 11am–1.30pm. Admission charge.

El Ghuri Wakala

This merchants' hostel and warehouse from the Mameluke period now serves as workshops for artisans and sells Bedouin crafts (*see p44*).

Sharia Mohammed Abduh, near El Azhar Mosque. 3km east of Midan el Tahrir. Tel: (202) 5107146. Open: 9am–5pm. Closed: Fri. Admission charge for exhibition area.

Facing page: View from the Cairo Tower, El Gezira
Below: The Mohammed Ali Mosque at the Citadel overlooks the entire city of Cairo

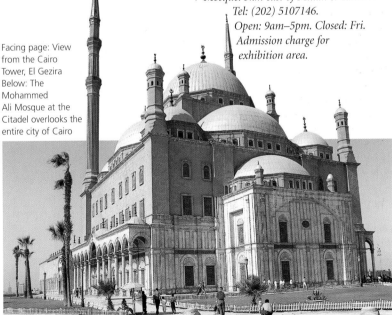

Ibn Tulun Mosque

One of the oldest and finest mosques in Cairo (*see p42*).
Restoration in progress but open to visit. Off Sharia el Salibah, 500m west of the Citadel. 3km southeast of Midan el Tahrir.
Open: 8am–6pm.
Admission charge.

Khan el Khalili

The wealth of Cairo was built on trade, and from all over Africa and Asia, caravans disgorged their cargoes for sale at the numerous bazaars that make up Khan el Khalili. Much of that medieval atmosphere still survives among the narrow covered passageways where you can join throngs of Cairenes who bargain over spices and perfume, oils, gold and silver jewellery, leather goods, and fabrics (*see p44*).

Within the northeast angle of Sharias el Muizz and el Muski, and spilling beyond as well. 3km east of Midan el Tahrir. Activity continues well on into the night.

Manyal Palace

Built in 1903 for Prince Mohammed Ali, brother of the Khedive Abbas II, this oriental, rococo-style palace set in a garden of banyan trees on Roda Island, is worth visiting for the opulence of its decoration and royal mementoes. The display includes a 1,000-piece silver service, a stuffed hermaphrodite goat, and a unique table made of elephants' ears.
Sharia Ahmed Abdel Rahim, Roda Island. 2km south of Midan el Tahrir. Tel: 3687495. Open: 9am–4pm. Admission charge.

El Muallaqa Church

This is popularly known as the Hanging Church because it is built atop the two walls of the Roman fortress (*see pp46–7*).
Old Cairo (Masr el Qadima). 4.5km south of Midan el Tahrir. Open: 8am–4pm. Free admission. Metro: Mari Girgis.

Nilometer

The 9th century Nilometer, a graduated column, measured the rise and fall of the Nile, and was built to determine the size of harvest, and what taxes should be imposed.
Southern tip of Roda Island. 4.5km south of Midan el Tahrir. Open: 9am–4pm. Closed: Fri. Admission charge.

THE MAMELUKES

As you walk through the streets of medieval Cairo (*see pp42–3*), you can still experience the atmosphere of *The Thousand and One Nights*. The tales were set in 9th-century Baghdad, but in reality they portray Cairo during the turbulent and spectacular Mameluke period (1250–1517).

The Mamelukes began as a slave militia, but they soon became an indispensable military elite who overthrew Salah el Din's dynasty. The Mamelukes saved Egypt from the Mongols and finished the task of driving the Crusaders from the Holy Land. Ruthless for power and often brutal, they nevertheless enriched Cairo with their bold and extravagant architecture, decorating its surfaces with intricate motifs and graceful arabesques. The mosque of Sultan Hassan and the mausoleum of Qaytbay are the two finest monuments from Mameluke times.

Qaytbay Mausoleum

The Eastern Cemetery (Qarafat el Sharqiyya), as the **City of the Dead** is properly known, is the burial place of several of the greatest Mameluke sultans, among them Qaytbay, whose mausoleum, completed in 1474, is one of the finest buildings in Cairo.

The exterior of the exquisitely proportioned dome is decorated with intricate reliefs of filigree flowers upon star-shaped polygons. The tomb chamber within is of immense height, its decoration breathtakingly variegated. The City of the Dead is far from being without life. The poor have always made their homes here, while relatives visit the more recent family tombs on feast days for a picnic.

East of Sharia Salah Salem. 1km east of El Azhar Mosque, 4km east of Midan el Tahrir. Open: 8am–4pm. Admission charge.

Rifai Mosque

A burial place of royalty (*see p43*).
Midan Salah el Din. 3km southeast of Midan el Tahrir. Open: 8am–4pm. Admission charge.

Sitt Barbara Church

A 7th-century Coptic church containing the relics of an early martyr (*see p47*).
Old Cairo (Masr el Qadima). 4.5km south of Midan el Tahrir. Open: 8am–4pm. Free admission. Metro: Mari Girgis.

Sultan Hassan Mosque

This is by far the finest Mameluke mosque in Cairo and regarded by many as the outstanding Islamic monument in Egypt (*see p43*).

Midan Salah el Din. 3km southeast of Midan el Tahrir. Open: 8am–5pm. Admission charge.

MUSEUMS OF CAIRO
Citadel Museums

The **Carriage Museum** contains six royal carriages, including one of gold. The **Military Museum** is filled less with hardware than with ceremonial bric-à-brac. The **National Police Museum** includes rooms devoted to Egypt's most famous murders and assassinations, though not that of President Sadat.

The **Khalil Museum** in Central Cairo has been renamed the **Ceramics Museum**. The Khalil art collection has been moved to the house where Sadat lived.

Aswân's ancient Nilometer, one of many throughout Egypt

Coptic Museum

This charming building, beautifully decorated with carved beams and *mashrabiyyas*, covers the period from the late Roman Empire through the early Middle Ages when Egypt was a largely Christian country. Its collection, gathered from churches and houses, links the art of the pharaonic and Graeco-Roman periods with that of Islam.

Attention is given to stonework, manuscripts, textiles, icons and paintings, woodwork, metalwork, pottery, and glass. The collection comprises folk art, often agreeably naive, though in textiles the Copts achieved a rare brilliance, weaving a delightful brightness and movement into their work (*see p46*).

Old Cairo (Masr el Qadima). 4.5km south of Midan el Tahrir. Tel: 3628766. Open: 9am–4pm. Closed: Fri 11am–1pm. Admission charge. Metro: Mari Girgis.

Museum of Egyptian Antiquities

This is a unique storehouse of one of the oldest and grandest civilisations on earth. The arrangement is more or less chronological, so that starting at the entrance and walking clockwise round the ground floor, you pass from Old Kingdom through Middle Kingdom and New Kingdom exhibits (the highlight on this floor is the Akhenaton room at the rear), concluding with Ptolemaic and Roman exhibits.

The first floor contains prehistoric and early dynastic exhibits and the contents of several tombs, most notably the magnificent array of wealth from Tutankhamun's. In the Mummy Room lie the bodies of such great pharaohs as Seti I and Ramses II.

Midan el Tahrir. Tel: 5754319. Open: 9am–4.45pm. Closed: Fri 11.15am–1.30pm. Admission charge, plus charge for the Mummy Room. The room housing Tutankhamun's treasures usually closes 30 minutes before the main museum. Metro: Sadat.

Islamic Art Museum

Your explorations of medieval Cairo will be greatly enriched by a visit to this museum, which contains many beautiful objects from the city's mosques and houses. Some of the displays group fountains, furniture, *mashrabiyyas*, and architectural decorations together, to recreate the atmosphere of a home or place of worship.

The collection is arranged in part chronologically, giving you a sense of Fatimid, Mameluke, and Ottoman styles, while some rooms are devoted to woodwork, metalwork, pottery, and manuscripts of all periods, and also include works of art from Turkey, Iraq, Persia, Spain, and China.

Intersection of Sharias Port Said and El Qa'la. 1.5km southeast of Midan el Tahrir. Tel: 3909930. Open: 9am–4pm. Closed: Fri 11.30am–1.30pm. Admission charge.

Agricultural Museum

Set within a beautiful garden of specimen trees, this is, in fact, three museums: the **Historical Museum** has displays of agricultural life in pharaonic times; the **Agricultural and Cotton Museum** concentrates on modern times, especially on Egypt's major cash crop;

and the **Natural History and Ethnological Museum** covers the animal life, hydrology, rural crafts, and culture of the Nile Valley and Delta.
At the western end of 6 October Bridge. 2km west of Midan el Tahrir. Tel: 7614999. Open: Tue–Sun 9am–2pm. Closed: Mon. Admission charge.

Papyrus Institute

Designed to preserve the ancient Egyptian art of papyrus-making, the institute contains a museum displaying the stages in the process. Sheets of papyrus can be purchased.

On a houseboat docked at Gîza's Corniche el Nil, near the Cairo Sheraton. 1.5km west of Midan el Tahrir. Tel: 5688627. Open: 10am–7pm. Free admission.

Railway Museum

This museum is for train buffs of all ages, with automated displays and old steam engines and carriages, including the Khedive Ismael's private train.
Midan Ramses, next to the main railway station. 2km northeast of Midan el Tahrir. Tel: 5763793. Open: Tue–Sun 8am–1pm. Closed: Fri noon, all day Mon. Admission charge.

The Mameluke Sultan Hassan Mosque

Walk: Ibn Tulun Mosque to the Citadel

This walk takes you to four famous mosques and the Gayer-Anderson House, and concludes with a sweeping view of Cairo.

Allow 3 hours.

SALADIN

Salah el Din, better known in the West as Saladin, was the chivalrous adversary of Richard the Lionheart during the Crusades. Of Kurdish stock, he became the champion of ortho-dox Sunni Islam, putting an end to Shi'ite Fatimid rule in Egypt and, after fortifying the Citadel, taking Jerusalem from the Crusaders in 1187.

Begin at the Ibn Tulun Mosque.

1 Ibn Tulun Mosque

In the 9th century, when the Arab world was ruled from Baghdad, Ibn Tulun was sent to govern Egypt. He borrowed the idea for the remarkable spiral minaret (which you can climb) from the Great Mosque of Samarra in Iraq. He also introduced the technique of carved stucco which adorns the arches around the vast central court. Designed as a congregational mosque to accommodate thousands of worshippers during Friday prayers, this is the finest example of its kind in Cairo. The impression is of severe simplicity, but you should walk round the court under the arcades to appreciate the rhythm of the arches and the play that is made with light and shadow (*see p38*).

Abutting the southeast corner of the mosque is the Gayer-Anderson House.

2 Gayer-Anderson House

See p37.

Walk east along Sharia el Salibah to Midan Salah el Din. At its north end, two large mosques stand close together. The nearest is the Sultan Hassan Mosque.

3 Sultan Hassan Mosque

This Mameluke mosque dating from the 1350s was reputedly built of stone taken from the Pyramid of Cheops. Its huge portal with stalactite decorations (a favourite Mameluke motif) leads you into a dark corridor from which you emerge into a brilliant sun-filled central court surrounded by magnificently soaring vaults, called *liwans*.

Unlike the Ibn Tulun Mosque, designed to be a great gathering place,

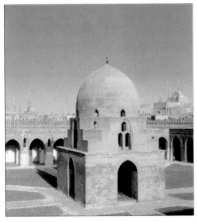

Courtyard of the Ibn Tulun Mosque

the Sultan Hassan was primarily a *madrasa* or theological school, the *liwans* serving as places of study. You should sit here a while, contemplating the wonderful interplay of dark and light, and how perfectly the open areas are set off by the built ones. Beyond the sanctuary *liwan* with its *mihrab* is Hassan's mausoleum (*see p39*).

Cross Sharia el Qa'la to the Rifai Mosque.

4 Rifai Mosque

Built in the early 20th century in mock-Mameluke style, the Rifai Mosque owes its fame to the tombs of several members of Mohammed Ali's dynasty, including King Farouk, who was deposed in 1952. The ex-Shah of Iran is also buried here (*see p39*).

Cross Midan Salah el Din to the base of the Citadel.

5 The Citadel

The western gate, Bab el Azab, is closed to the public. Here, Mohammed Ali massacred the Mamelukes in 1811, making himself absolute ruler of Egypt. Sent by the sultan in Istanbul to restore Ottoman authority after Napoleon's departure, his presence was resented by the Mamelukes. After inviting them to dinner at the Citadel, he locked the gate as they attempted to leave and shot them down with their bellies full.

Atop the Citadel (*see p36*) is the most familiar landmark in Cairo, the Mohammed Ali Mosque, famous also for its view. Looking westwards, you can trace your walk; the Rifai and Sultan Hassan mosques down below, and further off, the great rectangle of the Ibn Tulun Mosque.

Walk: Sharia el Muizz and Khan el Khalili

This walk takes you through the heart of the medieval city, the legendary world of *The Thousand and One Nights*. *Allow 3 hours.*

Begin at Bab Zuwayla.

1 Bab Zuwayla

Until the 19th century, medieval Cairo was encircled by 60 gates, of which only three remain. Eleventh-century Bab Zuwayla was the principal southern gate and the place of public executions.

Running north from the gate is Sharia el Muizz, the main street of the Fatimid city. The first building on the left is the 15th-century El Muayyad Mosque. From inside you can climb to the top of Bab Zuwayla for a fine view.
Continue north along Sharia el Muizz.

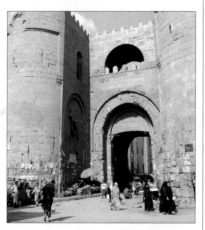

The imposing medieval gate of Bab Zuwayla

2 El Ghuri Madrasa, Mausoleum, and Wakala

Just before the intersection with Sharia el Azhar are the red-and-white-striped *madrasa* (left) and mausoleum (right) of the 16th-century Mameluke sultan El Ghuri. Whirling dervishes sometimes perform at the mausoleum. At the intersection turn right. After 100m is El Ghuri's *wakala*, the best preserved example of a merchants' hostel in Cairo (*see p37*).
Retrace your steps, cross Sharia el Azhar and continue north along Sharia el Muizz.

3 Khan el Khalili

There is the Spice Bazaar, on the edge of the vast warren that is Khan el Khalili (*see p38*). Turning right at the market street of Muski you come to the Per-fume Bazaar. Sharia el Muski continues east into a large square overlooked to the south by the 10th-century El Azhar Mosque (*see p34*), and to the north by Sayyidna el Hussein Mosque (non-Muslims not normally admitted).

To the west of the square is Fishawi's, a famous café where you can pause for refreshments (*see p169*).
From Sharia el Muski, walk 200m north along Sharia el Muizz.

4 Qalaun Madrasa and Mausoleum

On your left you see three domes, each with a stout minaret – a splendid cluster of religious buildings by the Mameluke sultans Qalaun, El Nasr, and Barquq. The finest of these complexes is the late 13th-century work of Qalaun. Inside, on the left, is the *madrasa* or theological school; on the right is Qalaun's mausoleum, a masterpiece of Mameluke architecture, richly ornamented beneath a soaring dome pierced by colourful stained-glass windows.

Walk north along Sharia el Muizz, then turn right into Haret el Darb el Asfar.

5 Bayt el Suhaymi

See pp35–6.

Continue north along Sharia el Muizz.

6 El Hakim Mosque

The 11th-century Fatimid Caliph el Hakim declared himself God and countered objections by chopping off heads and burning down half of Cairo. He was assassinated at the instigation of his sister.

For centuries, an aura of dread hung about the mosque, and it was allowed to crumble. It has now been restored and looks much brighter.

Walk: Coptic Cairo

This walk introduces you to some of the oldest churches in Egypt, as well as to its oldest synagogue.
Allow 1 hour, plus time for the museum.

Begin at the Mari Girgis metro station, facing the towers of the Roman fortress.

1 Roman Fortress

The section of wall and two towers are part of a Roman fortress which was built around 30 BC, after Augustus had defeated Antony and Cleopatra. The fortress once encompassed all the sites covered in this walk, but much of it was demolished by the British in the 19th century, leaving only these ruins.
After purchasing a ticket to the Coptic Museum and passing across its inner courtyard, you can descend to the level of the Roman water gate, into which the Nile still seeps, and step along raised walkways beneath arches and vaults. Above you is El Muallaqa Church.

2 Coptic Museum

The two Roman towers of the fortress also mark the entrance to the grounds of the Coptic Museum (*see p40*), its exhibits gathered from ancient churches and houses.
Leave between the Roman towers and turn left, following the walls round to the steps rising to the level of El Muallaqa.

3 El Muallaqa Church (Church of The Virgin)

This is popularly known as the Hanging Church because it is suspended on beams laid across the two bastions of the Roman water gate. It was probably built after the 7th-century Arab conquest, once the walls had become redundant. The interior is intricately decorated with pointed arches, cedar panelling, and translucent ivory screens. The carved marble pulpit is the finest in Egypt. On the right-hand wall is a 10th-

El Muallaqa, one of the oldest places of Christian worship in Egypt century icon of the Virgin and Child, and next to it an icon of St Mark, by tradition the founder of Christianity in Egypt (*see p38*).

Return to Sharia Mari Girgis, turn right, and follow the walls, passing the two Roman towers until you come to a small stairway which leads you to a passage through the walls. At the end of the street, turn right.

4 Abu Sarga Church (Church of St Sergius)

The Church of Abu Sarga, thought to date from the 5th century, is one of the oldest surviving churches in Egypt. According to tradition, the Holy Family found refuge in the crypt (once a cave), after their flight from Herod. Faded paintings of the apostles, probably 8th-century, adorn the columns of the nave, while 12th-century carved wooden panels on the altar screen depict the scenes of the Nativity and Last Supper (*see p34*).

Turn right out of Abu Sarga and then right at the corner. At the end of the street you see Sitt Barbara to the left.

5 Sitt Barbara Church (Church of St Barbara)

Built in the 7th century, its lofty wooden roof probably dates to Fatimid times. The relics of St Barbara are in the right-hand sanctuary. She had the misfortune, so legend goes, to be born in the 3rd century to a pagan father who, on discovering that she was a Christian, turned her over to the Roman authorities to be tortured and beheaded (*see p39*).

Turn left out of the church to the gateway crowned with the Star of David.

6 Ben Ezra Synagogue

This is the oldest synagogue in Egypt, restored in the 12th century by the Rabbi of Jerusalem, Abraham Ben Ezra, though probably converted from a church in the 9th century. A far older tradition claims that Jeremiah came here to preach after Nebuchadnezzar had destroyed Jerusalem in the 6th century BC (*see p36*).

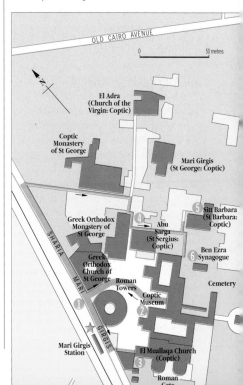

Cairo Environs

Around 3100 BC, Upper and Lower Egypt were united under the rule of Menes, who established the First Dynasty, and founded Memphis as his capital. Built only for the span of a lifetime, the palaces, shrines, and houses were made of mud brick. But at its necropolis of Saqqâra, the tombs of the dead were built of stone to endure eternity. Saqqâra was the world's first 'city' of stone. Some of its tombs, *mastabas*, resembled the single-storey houses of the living at Memphis, while the pharaoh Zoser had a grander idea. By placing a succession of ever smaller *mastabas* one on top of the other, he created his Step Pyramid. Subsequently, both to the north and south of Saqqâra, over 80 pyramids were constructed during the early Old Kingdom period, of which the Great Pyramids at Gîza are the largest and most famous.

GÎZA PYRAMIDS COMPLEX

At the western edge of Gîza, 11km west of Cairo. The complex includes the Pyramids, the Sphinx, and Chephren's Valley Temple. Open: daily 7am–4pm; site remains open until 8pm in winter, midnight in summer. Admission charge. **Solar Boat Museum**: Open: daily 7am– 3.30pm. Admission charge. (*For the* **Sound and Light** *performances, see p50*).

GÎZA PYRAMIDS COMPLEX

The long straight road from Cairo passes through the built-up suburb of Gîza and finally curves sharply to the left and mounts the desert plateau. Alternatively, take the Ming road, following signs for the Pyramids. Once at the site, before you is the Pyramid of Cheops, the oldest and largest of the three Gîza Pyramids. Beyond stand the pyramids of Chephren and Mycerinus, in descending order of age and size along a southwest axis, each identically oriented 8.5 degrees west of magnetic north. Built between 2600 BC and 2525 BC, they were probably aligned precisely with the North Star.

Near the edge of the desert, and accessible by boat during the inundation

Pyramid of Cheops

King's Chamber
Air shafts
Great Gallery
Queen's Chamber
Ascending passage
Level passage
Descending passage
Height: 137.2m
Original height: 146.5m
Base: 230sq.m
Unfinished Chamber
CROSS SECTION

was a modest valley chapel. From here a walled-in causeway led up to the funerary temple on the east side of the pyramid, where the soul of the dead pharaoh could emerge from its tomb to partake of the offered feasts. Not all of these structures have survived. On the sides of the Pyramid of Cheops, wooden solar boats have been found in pits (*see p50*), and there are smaller pyramids, some for royal wives, as well as rows of flat-topped tombs called *mastabas* for nobles and royal princes.

Pyramid of Cheops

Once, all the pyramids had smooth sides of polished stone, but the casing on the Pyramid of Cheops has entirely gone, and you see instead the underlying tiered courses of 2,500,000 limestone blocks. Inside, a descending corridor reaches a chamber in the bedrock, left unfinished, possibly because of flooding, while a detour off the ascending corridor leads to the so-called Queen's Chamber. Far grander is the ascending Great Gallery, which leads to the King's Chamber. On the north and south walls of this, a metre above the floor, you can see the ventilation shafts which reach to the surface of the pyramid. The weight of 95m of

pyramid sits above your head, but the pressure is redirected away from the burial chamber by five successive relieving chambers above the granite roofing slabs. Cheops' name was found inscribed in the relieving chambers; otherwise, the King's Chamber contains neither inscriptions nor decorations, and its sarcophagus was found empty.

The Great Pyramid of Cheops

Cheops' funerary solar boat found in perfect condition displays intricate craftsmanship

Pyramid of Chephren

Chephren's Pyramid is almost as large as Cheops', and seems larger as it stands on higher ground. The impression of greater height is also due to the casing stones which are intact towards the top. Its interior, however, is less interesting. Its tomb chamber also contained an empty sarcophagus. All three pyramids seemed sealed when entered during the 19th century. In fact, each had been looted at some ancient time.

Pyramid of Mycerinus

At 66.5m in height, this is the smallest of the three main pyramids. A 9th-century caliph attempted to demolish the pyramids altogether, starting with that of Mycerinus. Eight months and 170,000 blocks of stone later, he gave up, leaving the gouge you see on the north face.

Solar Boat Museum

Some say that solar boats were built to ferry the pharaoh as he followed the sun god across the skies. Five solar boat pits have been found round the base of the Pyramid of Cheops. The first three were empty, but in 1954 and 1987, two dismantled but perfectly preserved boats of Syrian cedar were discovered. The latter has been left within its pit, but the former, 4,600 years old and 43m long, has been reassembled and put on display in the specially-built museum at the south face of the Pyramid of Cheops.

Sound and Light

The Sphinx plays the dramatic role of narrator in this booming and atmospheric programme telling the story of the Pyramids. Bring a sweater; even in summer the evenings can get cool.

The Sphinx

A limestone outcrop was left standing in the quarry from which many of the blocks for Cheops' Pyramid were cut. His son Chephren had the idea of shaping it into a figure with a lion's body and a god's face – although perhaps the face is Chephren's own. The Turks used the Sphinx for target practice in the 16th century and shot off its nose. The beard is at the British Museum. Though 20m high and 48.5m long, the Sphinx may not seem as large as you might imagine, as much of its bulk crouches within the quarry. The poor quality of its stone has contributed to its erosion.

Valley Temple of Chephren
By the south flank of the Sphinx, Chephren's valley temple has been well preserved by its long burial under the sands. Majestically assembled from pink Aswân granite, its square monolithic pillars support massive architraves. Some authorities think Chephren's mummification took place here; it is more generally agreed that this is where the 'Opening of the Mouth' ceremony took place, the *ka* or soul of the pharaoh entering and leaving his body.

> ### Sound and Light
> The Sound and Light pavilion faces the Sphinx and is signposted left off the main road to the Pyramids, 1km before the Mena House Oberoi, 10km west of Cairo's Midan el Tahrir (*tel: (202) 3852880/3863469*). There are two evening performances – 6.30pm and 7.30pm (times differ according to season), as follows: Mon: English and French; Tue: French and Italian; Wed: English and French; Thu: Arabic and English; Fri: English and French; Sat: English and Spanish; Sun: French and German. Admission charge.

Pyramids of Gîza

MEMPHIS

Most probably beginning as a fortress from which Menes controlled the land and water routes between Upper and Lower Egypt, Memphis was the capital of the country throughout the Old Kingdom period. Though New Kingdom Egypt was ruled from Thebes, the former capital remained a great city until overtaken by Ptolemaic Alexandria. Centuries of Nile mud have since swallowed Memphis, and there is now little to see.

Colossus of Ramses II

The New Kingdom pharaoh Ramses II was one

Impressive statue of Ramses II

of those who continued to embellish Memphis with great buildings and statues, including a pair of colossal statues of himself which probably stood outside the Temple of Ptah.

Hauled out of the mud in 1820, one now stands outside the main Cairo railway station, and the other was offered to the British Museum – which failed to collect. So here it lies, flat on its back, specially encased within a modern building. Other smaller statues stand or lie about in the surrounding gardens, including a large alabaster sphinx from the New Kingdom period.

Mummification Beds

Across the road from the garden with its sphinx are the alabaster mummification beds where the bodies of the Apis bulls were soaked in a liquid containing natron (a natural salt) to dehydrate them in preparation for burial (*see* Serapeum, *pp54–5*).

Temple of Ptah

The faint remains of this temple to the venerated god of Memphis lie waterlogged near the mummification beds.

MEMPHIS

The ruins of Memphis are at the village of Mit Rahina, 3km from El Badrashein, on the west bank of the Nile, south of Cairo. Memphis is 32km south of Cairo by road, 21km south of the Gîza Pyramids, and 6km southeast of Saqqâra. It is included in most tours to Saqqâra; otherwise the only practical way of getting here is by hiring a taxi.
Open: daily 8am–5pm (4pm in winter).
Admission charge.

SAQQÂRA

Saqqâra is on the desert plateau above Memphis, 30km south of Cairo by road, 19km south of the Gîza Pyramids, and 6km northwest from Memphis. The only practical ways of getting here are by guided tour or taxi, or by horse or camel across the desert from the Gîza Pyramids (*see p48*).
Open: daily 8am–5pm (4pm in winter).
Admission charge.

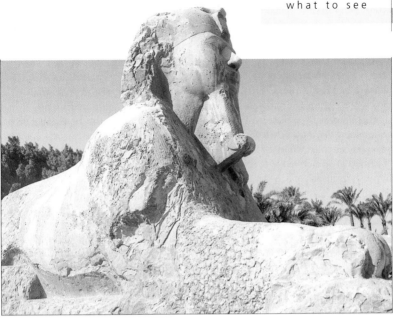

The 18th-century BC alabaster sphinx at Memphis, surrounded by palm-lined pathways

SAQQÂRA

The sands wash about your feet nearly everywhere at Saqqâra which has more of a desert feel about it than Gîza. Named after Sokkar, the Memphite god of the dead, this was a necropolis for over 3,000 years, though most of its greatest monuments belong to the Old Kingdom. It was here that the ancient Egyptians first put into practice on a grand scale their attempt to defeat time – by replacing the perishable mud brick of their homes and shrines at Memphis with eternal replicas in stone.

Mastaba of Akhti-Hotep and Ptah-Hotep

Belonging to the priest Ptah-Hotep and his father, the vizier Akhti-Hotep, this 5th-Dynasty double *mastaba* is outstanding for the variety and quality of its coloured reliefs.

The entrance corridor has reliefs in progress. The preliminary drawings are in red, and the master's corrections in black. Across a pillared hall you enter Ptah-Hotep's tomb chamber. A relief on the right wall shows Ptah-Hotep in the panther-skin of a high priest, seated at a cornucopian offering table, a goblet raised to his lips. A catalogue of daily events fills the left wall, including boys and girls playing games and a cow giving birth. The details are vivid: notice, for example, the hare emerging from its hole with a cricket in its mouth. Above the entrance you see Ptah-Hotep preparing for the day. A manicurist works at his hands, a pedicurist at his feet, musicians are entertaining him, with dogs and a pet monkey nearby. Across the pillared hall is the similar, but less finely decorated, tomb chamber of Akhti-Hotep.

Mastaba of Mereruka

Mereruka was vizier to a 6th-Dynasty pharaoh and his 32-room *mastaba* is the largest at Saqqâra. The entry passage shows him painting a picture of the seasons and playing a board game to pass away eternity, while the first three chambers are decorated with scenes of hunting, furniture-making, and goldsmiths at work. At the far end of the *mastaba*, in a chapel with six pillars, is a statue of Mereruka himself. The scenes to the left of this show the domestication of gazelles, goats, and hyenas.

Mastaba of Ti

Ti was overseer of royal farms and mortuary temples in the 5th Dynasty. He was also the royal hairdresser.

The reliefs in Ti's beautifully decorated funerary chamber rival those of Ptah-Hotep's, and exceed them in variety. The highlight here is a relief of

Saqqâra

Ti sailing through the marshes. The scene is full of symbolism, for this is Ti fighting against the forces of evil as represented by the hunted hippopotamus, and of chaos represented by the fish and birds. The crocodile, at once being bitten by and biting the hippopotamus, was sacred and represents good.

Through a slot in the far wall, in the *serdab* (closed corridor with statues of the dead), you can see a statue of Ti. Here his soul or *ka* awaited the offerings brought to the chamber. You will notice that his hair, or wig, is well done.

Pyramid of Unas

Unas was the last pharaoh of the 5th Dynasty, and the 350 years from the Step Pyramid through the Great Pyramids at Gîza to this heap of rubble mark the rise and fall of the Old Kingdom sun cult. Unfortunately, its core was shoddily built of loose stone and rubble; the pyramid is not safe to enter. The tomb chamber is entirely covered with inscriptions celebrating eternal life and the newly-popular resurrection cult of Osiris.

The Serapeum

The Serapeum, where the Apis bulls were buried, is the strangest place at Saqqâra. Long, gloomily-lit, rock-cut galleries beneath the desert are lined with gigantic vaults, each vault containing a bull-sized black sarcophagus. For generations, these Apis bulls were buried like kings, for they were believed to be incarnations of Ptah, the god of Memphis. The oldest galleries date back to Ramses II, although those

Zoser's 'stairway to heaven'

open to the public belong to the period of the Ptolemies. (*See* Mummification Beds, *p52*.)

Step Pyramid of Zoser

The Step Pyramid is the central piece of an extensive funerary complex built for the 3rd-Dynasty pharaoh Zoser, who lived around 2700 BC. Surrounded by an enclosure wall probably built in imitation of the city walls of Memphis, this first pyramid, 62m high, was created by placing a series of ever smaller *mastabas* one on top of the other.

The Great South Court, with its frieze of cobras, and the shrines in the Heb-Sed Court next to it, represent the ritual Heb-Sed race run in Memphis by the pharaoh during his 30th jubilee celebrations, impressing and reinvigorating a united Upper and Lower Egypt with his spiritual strength.

There is a relief of Zoser running the Heb-Sed race in the South Tomb, which is decorated with blue faïence tiles. It is reached via a deep shaft.

Passing along the east side of the Step Pyramid you come to the House of the South, its lotus capitals symbolising Upper Egypt, and the House of the North, with papyrus capitals on its graceful columns to symbolise Lower Egypt. Against the north side of the pyramid is the *serdab*, in which stands a *ka* statue of Zoser. His eyes are forever fixed on the North Star, the star which never sets and so never dies.

Part of the extensive Sed Festival complex at Zoser's Step Pyramid

Desert Ride: Gîza to Saqqâra

This journey across the desert and along the edge of the cultivated zone can be done by either horse or camel. It allows you to see several rarely visited pyramids and sun temples along the way. A camel will cost more to hire than a horse. Most people, however, will find a horse more comfortable over this distance. Outside summer bring something warm to wear; the desert can get very windy and chilly.

Allow 3 hours in each direction, plus time to look around Saqqâra. Or, ride to Saqqâra and return to Gîza by taxi.

Start from the stables behind the Sound and Light pavilion, which is the best place to hire your mount.

1 Pyramids of Gîza

You pass a modern Muslim cemetery on your left and then head south across the sands. To the east you will see the cultivated zone of the Nile Valley. The encroaching outskirts of Cairo soon disappear from sight and behind you there is a wonderful view of the Gîza Pyramids (*see pp48–51*), which belong to the 3rd-Dynasty period, standing alone on the desert plateau.

After about an hour and a quarter you come to two pyramids.

2 Pyramids of Zawiyat el Aryan

The northerly Unfinished Pyramid, abandoned during the 4th Dynasty some time after the Gîza Pyramids, is surrounded by unused granite and limestone blocks. Fifteen minutes to the southeast, and nearer the cultivation, is the **Layer Pyramid**, older than those at Gîza though it belongs to the 3rd Dynasty. Built of small blocks, it was perhaps meant to be a step pyramid. *About half an hour south, near the cultivation (where roses are the local speciality), are two sun temples.*

3 Abu Ghurab Sun Temples

The sun was always venerated by the ancient Egyptians. It is said that pyramids and obelisks, with a pyramid-shape at the top and sometimes covered with gold and silver, imitated the sun's rays spreading across the earth. In the courtyard of the northerly 5th-Dynasty **Sun Temple of Nyuserre** stand an altar and the base of a solar obelisk. The obelisk has vanished, but you can climb up within the base for views across the desert.

Immediately to the southeast, passing by the Sun Temple of Userkaf, are the pyramids of Abusir.

4 Abusir Pyramids

The northernmost **Pyramid of Sahure** is badly damaged, though you can crawl through a narrow passage into its tomb chamber and also climb to the summit. From here there is a fine panorama of the other 5th-Dynasty pyramids in this

cluster and their attendant mortuary temples. The group is named after the nearby village.

Continuing on, you pass the pyramids of **Nyuserre**, **Neferikare**, and **Neferefre**. Neither the first nor last of these was ever finished owing to the early deaths of their pharaohs.

Neferikare also died early, but work continued, although what had begun with red granite and limestone was completed in mud brick.

Abusir is not always open to the public. Hours are 8am–4pm. Admission charge.

5 Approaching Saqqâra

You can now clearly see the Step Pyramid and other structures at Saqqâra (*see pp53–5*), no more than half an hour's ride south, and beyond that the **Red Pyramid** and the **Bent Pyramid** at Dahshur, both built by a 4th-Dynasty pharaoh, together with another pyramid now collapsed. *Dahshur is usually open: 8am–4pm. Admission charge.*

Both the camel and its owner proudly solicit your custom

Excursions from Cairo

THE DELTA

Whatever your interest in its ancient sites, there is fascination in a drive or train ride through the green and watery landscape of the Nile Delta, the river's last great outpouring before it reaches the Mediterranean Sea. The area is extraordinarily flat, and the sky is vast. The sails of feluccas billow amid fields furrowed by canals. Buffalo turn wheels for grinding or pumping, and brightly coloured figures move through an abundance of cotton, rice, and maize.

In antiquity the Nile had seven arms here. Now it has only two. One flows into the Mediterranean Sea at Dumyât (Damietta), the other flows out at Rashid (Rosetta). As all the other tributaries dried up or changed course, cities were abandoned, often then disappearing beneath the mud. In Upper Egypt, where the river has been confined to its narrow valley, much of the past has been preserved. In the Delta, history has too often been erased. Yet the Delta knew greatness. From their capital in the Eastern Delta, the Hyksos, a foreign people of uncertain origin, ruled over the whole of Egypt during the 2nd Intermediate Period, and in the Eastern Delta, too, was the Land of Goshen mentioned in *Genesis* and *Exodus*.

The dynasty of Seti I had its roots in the Delta, and his son, Ramses II, built his northern capital, Pi-Ramses, here. Throughout the first millennium BC the Delta dominated the affairs of Egypt – various dynasties had their capitals at Tanis, Bubastis, and Sais. The Delta's importance became all the greater when the Ptolemies built their capital at Alexandria.

Bubastis

Near Zagazig, Bubastis is one of the most ancient sites in Egypt. The name means House of the Goddess Bastet, who was represented as a lioness, and later as a graceful cat. the ruins of her temple, founded during the Old Kingdom but rebuilt during the 22nd Dynasty, can be seen here. Beneath it are galleries for the burial of cats.

VISITING

Like the arms of the Nile itself, the principal roads and railway lines fan out northwards from Cairo, while links between the Eastern and Western Delta are poor. The Western Delta can be visited en route to Alexandria, which is linked to Cairo by the main railway line and the Agricultural Road, while **Rashid** (Rosetta – *see* p75) should be visited from Alexandria itself. Sites in the Eastern Delta are best visited by making a loop around Zagazig, while Dumyât would be a separate excursion.

3km south of Zagazig, along the road to Bilbeis. Open: daily 9am–4pm. Free admission. Service taxis (which will drop you off at Bubastis), buses, and trains all run the 80km from Cairo to Zagazig.

Dumyât (Damietta)

Situated 15km from the Mediterranean on a narrow strip of land between the eastern arm of the Nile and Lake Manzala, Dumyât is a thriving port and industrial centre, preserving numerous mansions from the Ottoman period. Bird-watchers are attracted to the lake, which is, in fact, a brackish lagoon reaching eastwards towards Port Said.

Famous at the time of the Crusades as Damietta, St Louis of France landed here in 1249, but was captured and ransomed. During an earlier attack on the city in 1218, St Francis of Assisi courageously crossed enemy lines and offered to enter a fiery furnace on the condition that should he come out alive, the sultan and his people would convert to Christianity. The sultan replied by giving the saint a lesson in humanity and common sense, saying that gambling with one's life was not a valid proof of one's God.

210km northeast of Cairo and served by train and bus.

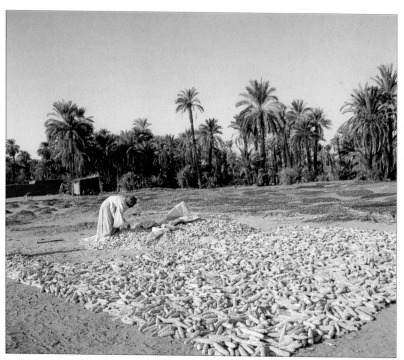

Drying and cleaning corn prior to packaging

Pi-Ramses

Mentioned in *Exodus 1:11* and *12:37* as the city built for the pharaoh by the afflicted children of Israel, and as their point of departure out of Egypt under Moses' leadership, the site of Pi-Ramses is thought to be marked by the negligible ruins found at Qantir.
Qantir, near Faqus. 45km northeast of Zagazig.

Sais

Though at times the capital during the Late Dynastic Period, there is nothing to see today at Sais. The site has suffered from the activities of the *sebakhin*, and is an interesting example of how Egypt lives upon its past. In a land where wood is a rarity and animal dung has long been used for fuel, the *fellahin* have turned to the debris mounds or *koms* of ancient towns. These yield a rich soil called *sebakh* which is used as a fertiliser. The once royal city of Sais is now a waterlogged depression.
30km to the northwest of Tanta.

Tanis

Egyptologists once argued that Tanis was the site of Pi-Ramses. Though this impressive lineage is now disputed, the fact that these are the most impressive ruins in the Delta region cannot be denied.

The **Temple of Amun** is spectacular for its fallen

A Bedouin from Siwa Oasis

THE TANTA MOULID

The *moulid* at Tanta is not linked, like so many other Muslim festivals, to the lunar calendar, but is fixed to coincide with the autumn harvest, a time of joy. During the festival large quantities of sugar-coated nuts called *hubb el Azziz* (seeds of the Beloved Prophet) are consumed – a favourite delicacy since ancient times.

A burlesque side-show accompanies the more serious ritual of the *moulid*, known locally as *zeffa el Sharamit*, the procession of the prostitutes. In the past, barges full of boisterous men and women would draw close to riverbank towns so that the women could 'shout abuse at the women of the place or start dancing, or stand up and hitch up their skirts'.

colossal statuary, and you can enter the royal tombs of its 21st- and 22nd-Dynasty pharaohs, whose capital this was. The splendid gold masks, inlaid jewellery, and silver sarcophagus discovered here in 1939, and rivalling the treasures of Tutankhamun, are now in the Egyptian Antiquities Museum in Cairo (*see p40*). A sacred lake and the remains of two other temples are evident within the enclosure walls.
Near San el Hagar. 74km northeast of Zagazig. Some tours come here, otherwise take a taxi and have it wait for you. Open: daily 9am–4pm. Admission charge.

Tanta

This nondescript city, with a population of over 250,000, is Egypt's fifth largest. It jumps to life at the end of the October cotton harvest, when as many as two million people, from all round the Arab world, attend the joyous *moulid* centred round the mosque and tomb of a 13th-century Sufi saint, Said Ahmed el Badawi (*see box*).
90km northwest of Cairo, on the railway line to Alexandria.

Zagazig

Dating only from the 1820s, this is the birthplace of Ahmed Orabi, leader of the 1882 revolt against British influence. Zagazig is a good place to begin a tour of the Eastern Delta. Its Orabi Museum contains objects from nearby Bubastis.
85km northeast of Cairo from where it is well served by various types of transport: taxi, bus and train. Orabi Museum open: 9am–1pm. Closed: Tue.

A boisterous carnival atmosphere prevails at the *moulid*

The Faiyûm and the Western Desert

THE FAIYÛM

Although almost entirely surrounded by the Western Desert, the Faiyûm is not a true oasis because it depends on the Nile. Failure to maintain the Faiyûm's irrigation system during the late Roman period caused Lake Qarun to shrink, leaving ghost towns all round its desert perimeter (*see pp64–5*).

Revival began under the British, and the Faiyûm now possesses 2,300km of capillary canals – equal to the entire length of the Nile through Egypt. Cereals, fruit, and flowers grow again in wonderful profusion, and increasing numbers of visitors are attracted to the Faiyûm as much for its rural charm as for its ancient sites.

Kom Aushim (Ancient Karanis)

Offering a good panorama of the lake and oasis from the rim of the Faiyûm depression, Karanis is the most accessible of the abandoned Ptolemaic towns. Beyond the roadside museum are ancient streets and houses,

and two temples dedicated to crocodile gods.

Served by buses and service taxis plying the desert road between Cairo (76km) and Medinet el Faiyûm (30km). Museum open: 9am–4pm. Closed: Mon. Admission charge.

Medinet el Faiyûm

All roads and canals radiate from this ordinary market centre, site of the Ptolemaic city of Crocodilopolis.

Obelisk of Sesostris I

This 12th-Dynasty obelisk, now pieced together, stands at a roundabout as you arrive from Cairo.

Qaytbay Mosque

This Mameluke mosque (AD 1476), which has columns from ancient Crocodilopolis, is a 10-minute walk west from the tourist office at the centre of town.

Souk

Near the Qaytbay Mosque is a warren of market streets selling food, spices, copperware, jewellery, and a variety of *bric-à-brac*.

THE FAIYÛM

100km southwest of Cairo. The Faiyûm is reached by bus or service taxi to Medinet el Faiyûm. It is possible you may have to have a police escort (*see p187*).

OASES OF THE WESTERN DESERT

With the exception of Siwa near the Libyan border, which is reached by travelling west from Alexandria to Mersa Matruh and then south, the oases of the Western Desert are linked by a 1,000km road looping out from Cairo and back to the Nile at Asyût. All can be reached by bus and service taxi. It is possible you may have to have a police escort (*see p187*). There are flights to Khârga.

Waterwheels

Four waterwheels groan away outside the Cafeteria el Medina by the tourist office at the centre of town. There are 200 throughout the oasis. In 30 minutes you can walk to the Seven Waterwheels, a Faiyûm landmark, north of town.

OASES OF THE WESTERN DESERT
Baharîya

White-walled houses and a 6th-century Coptic church mark the old quarter of **Bawiti** on a ridge, Qarat el-Farargi, overlooking palm groves. One kilometre west is the sister village of **El Qasr**, its houses incorporating stones from a 26th-Dynasty temple and a Roman arch. A recent discovery is the Mummies Valley which is not open to the public. Four mummies can, however, be seen at the local museum.
Open 9am–4pm. Free admission.

Dakhla

Dakhla is the most beautiful of the oases. Its two main towns are **Mut**, with hot springs nearby at **Mut Talata** and, 27km to the west, **El Qasr**, the original fortified settlement of the oasis which has a Mameluke mosque and a Roman temple close by.

Farafra

Isolated Farafra has a picturesque old quarter and walled palm groves for delightful walks. The atmosphere is religiously conservative.

El Khârga

El Khârga town is a developed and unromantic place, although at ancient **Hibis**, on its northern outskirts, there is a temple of Amun, and one kilometre beyond at **Baqawat**, there is an early Christian necropolis.

Siwa

The well-preserved temple of Amun rises from vast groves of date palms and fruit trees. Here, Alexander came to consult the oracle and was told he was a god. Siwa continues to deliver romance, and although its crumbling fortified village has been abandoned for newer houses, traditions remain strong. Veiled women drape themselves in silver jewellery, Berber is spoken instead of Arabic, and local festivals and marriage customs are still observed – though homosexual marriage was discontinued earlier this century.

The water-wheel is an age old method of irrigation

Tour: The Faiyûm

When in late Roman times the irrigation system of the Faiyûm began to fail through neglect, a number of Ptolemaic towns and more ancient sites around the periphery of the oasis were abandoned to the advancing sands. Medinet el Faiyûm is the transport hub from which to start each visit. The tourist office at the centre of town, by the café with the four waterwheels, can give you information on different means of touring this area.

Allow 1 day if you have a car. By public transport, select one or two sights to visit. Be prepared to have a police escort.

The direct route to Lake Qarun is via Sanhur. From here, you can approach the Auberge du Lac from the east or by way of the lakeside village of Shakshuk.

1 Auberge du Lac

The Auberge du Lac was originally King Farouk's hunting lodge, but is now a hotel, crowded on weekends. From its veranda you can look out over the lake, which attracts great numbers of

Remains of a mud-brick town

migratory birds, including the pink flamingo, and thousands of ducks. *From here or Shakshuk you can hire a boatman for an hour's journey across the lake to Dimeh el Siba.*

2 Dimeh el Siba

In Ptolemaic times this was a lakeside town called Soknopaios Nesos. Now you must walk up a steep 3km track from the north shore of the lake to reach this scene of majestic desolation.

A 400m processional way begins at what was the lakeshore and passes through the town gate to the **Temple of Soknopaios and Isis** with several reliefs, one of Ptolemy II praying before Amun. The settlement was a fortified caravan station from where the long journey across the desert to distant oases began. *There are service taxis from the Auberge du Lac, Shakshuk, and Medinet el Faiyûm to Ibshaway, then on to the village of Qasr Qarun near the western extremity of the lake.*

3 Qasr Qarun

Beside the village are the remains of the
Ptolemaic settlement of **Dionysias**, its
most notable feature a sandstone
Ptolemaic temple dedicated to the
crocodile god Sobek. You can explore its
labyrinthine interior, and climb up to
the roof for distant views over the oasis
and desert.

To reach ancient Narmouthis, known
as Medinet Madi, take a bus to Menshat
Sef, a village south of Abu Gandir.
Walking west from here, follow the
canal, cross over the first bridge, and
take the narrow track south. Within
an hour you will see a stone hut on
the desert's rise. Just beyond it is
Medinet Madi.

4 Medinet Madi

A processional way lined by lions and
sphinxes approaches the 12th-Dynasty
temple dedicated to Sobek which is
covered with numerous reliefs. The
mud-brick remains of the town lie
about, while an embankment to the
north of the temple was in fact the
storm beach of Lake Qarun.

Wadi Natrûn

The Coptic monasteries of the Wadi Natrûn, once isolated in the Western Desert, now lie within sight of the 200km Desert Road built between Cairo and Alexandria in the 1930s. Founded early in the 4th century, they are among the oldest monasteries in the world. They look like fortresses, their great walls surrounding a central keep built in defence against Bedouin raids. Often rebuilt both within and without, nothing stands from before the period of the 7th century. Today, these and other desert monasteries are at the heart of the spiritual revival of the Coptic Church, and their monks are recruited from the universities and the professions.

Monastery of St Baramus (Deir el Baramus)

Parts of the monastery Church of el Adra (the Virgin) date from the 9th

Monastery of the Syrians

century, and alongside is the old refectory. From the 11m-high walls you can look down into the monastery's arbour-shaded courtyard, and out into the surrounding desert where hermits' caves can be seen.

Monastery of St Bishoi (Deir Anba Bishoi)

From his tomb in the 9th-century Church of St Bishoi, the saint himself is said occasionally to reach out and shake the hands of believers. The atmosphere suggested by the tale, however, has been stripped away by much modern rebuilding, making this the least interesting of the four monasteries.

GETTING TO THE MONASTERIES

From the Rest House, 95km northwest of Cairo on the Desert Road to Alexandria, a road runs 3km to Bir Hooker village. There the road forks, right 12km for the Monastery of Baramus, left 7km for the monasteries of the Syrians and St Bishoi.

The Monastery of St Makarius is most easily reached from the Desert Road: 82km north of Cairo, a road runs west for 8km to the monastery. Buses and service taxis running between Cairo and Alexandria stop at the Rest House, where you can hire a local taxi. Alternatively, hire a taxi from Cairo for the day.

All four monasteries are generally open daily from 9am to 5pm, but some or all may be fully or partly closed during periods of fasting. Visitors to the Monastery of St Makarius need a letter of introduction from the Coptic Patriarch in Cairo. (See pp178–9 for details on visiting and staying overnight.)

Monastery of St Makarius (Deir Abu Maqar)

You might almost think this a holiday village for monks when you enter the monastery courtyard surrounded by new cells, a refectory, library, guesthouse, bakery, and other amenities. Much of ancient interest still survives.

In the large Church of St Makarius, the 7th-century domed sanctuary of John the Baptist is decorated with a winged cherub and the four horses of the Apocalypse. On the arch before the sanctuary are finely painted 11th-century scenes of Christ's burial. The three-storey keep, entered by a drawbridge, is also 11th-century. There are four churches within it, with wonderful paintings on their walls.

Monastery of the Syrians (Deir el Suryani)

With a huge hull supporting a super-structure of domes, towers, and crosses, this most fascinating of the four monasteries is like a great ship riding the waves of desert sand.

The 10th-century Church of el Adra (the Virgin) in the complex is remarkable for the decorative doors facing the sanctuary, and more so for the beautiful frescos in the semidomes of the choir.

On the right are the Annunciation and Nativity; on the left, the Dormition of the Virgin. At the opposite end of the church is a grotto, said to have been the hermit's cell of St Bishoi built long before the church.

Fresco of the Annunciation in the Church of el Adra, Monastery of the Syrians

Alexandria

Alexandria is Egypt's major port and the country's second largest city, with a population of over four million. Unlike the rest of the country, it is cool and wet in winter, with refreshing Mediterranean breezes during the heat of summer. Alexander the Great founded the city in 332 BC on the site of a small fishing village, Rhakotis. He then built a causeway connecting the island of Pharos (where Ras el Tin Palace and Qaytbay Fort stand) to the mainland, creating two great harbours which became the basis of Alexandria's prosperity.

A mummy with Christian cross

This spirit of invention was continued under Alexander's Greek successors, the Ptolemies, who built the famous Pharos lighthouse, established the Great Library, and founded the Mouseion, a research institute where remarkable advances were made in mathematics, engineering, and medicine. Later still,

Alexandria played a formative role in the development of Christian thought, adding Greek philosophy to Jewish and Egyptian beliefs.

Little of this ancient and illustrious city survives, however. After the 7th-century Arab invasion, Alexandria declined. Refounded early in the 19th

Alexandria

century by Mohammed Ali, foreigners were attracted by the promise of trading opportunities, especially in cotton. Cosmopolitan and lively, the city enjoyed a gilded age through to the 1950s, its hothouse atmosphere captured vividly in Lawrence Durrell's *Alexandria Quartet*. Now somewhat provincial and down-at-heel despite a face-lift, the city possesses little glamour and few ancient sites, but Alexandria's situation is charming, and its past still haunts the fading streets. Very crowded in summer, better in winter.

Abu el Abbas and Bouseiri Mosques

The domes and minarets of these adjacent mosques lend a graceful touch to the skyline of the Eastern Harbour (*see p73*). The larger of the two is the Abu el Abbas Mosque, built in 1943 over a 13th-century tomb. Around it clusters the picturesque old quarter. Between it and the Corniche is the Bouseiri

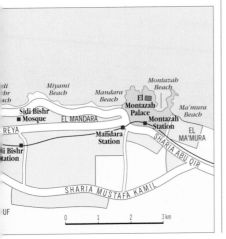

Mosque, twinkling with lights at night. *Overlooking the Corniche towards Qaytbay Fort. 2km northwest of Midan Sa'ad Zaghloul. Open: dawn until late. Free admission.*

Anfushi Tombs

Cut into the limestone ridge that formed the island of Pharos, these four tombs are basically Greek with Egyptian elements. The walls are painted to give the impression of marble and tile. In the tomb furthest to the right there are scenes of a *felucca*, and a warship of the type Cleopatra might have used to sail in to Actium.
At the western end of Sharia Ras el Tin. 2.5km northwest of Midan Sa'ad Zaghloul. Open: daily 9am–4pm. Closed: Fri 11.30am–1.30pm. Admission charge.

Attarine

There is everything from old postcards to antique furniture to fascinate you in this flea market area of Alexandria, which centres on Sharia el Attarine. *Sharia el Attarine runs south from Sharia Sidi el Mitwalli. 1km south of Midan Sa'ad Zaghloul. Shops open until 9pm.*

Coptic Orthodox Cathedral of St Mark

The interior of the church is handsome. Note the plaque listing all the Coptic patriarchs, going right back to St Mark, said to be the traditional founder of Christianity in Egypt.
Rue de l'Eglise Copte, west along Sharia Sa'ad Zaghloul from Sharia el Nebi Danyal. 400m southwest from Midan Sa'ad Zaghloul. Open: early morning until late. Free admission.

Graeco-Roman Museum

Filling the historical gap between the Egyptian Antiquities Museum and the Coptic Museum, both in Cairo, the Graeco-Roman Museum covers the fascinating period when Western culture overlaid and sometimes incorporated the native Egyptian world. Its spacious and uncluttered rooms are arranged around a central garden, making it a pleasant place to linger. Many of the exhibits are from Alexandria and its vicinity; the rest are from other areas of Greek settlement – the Delta, the Faiyûm, and Middle Egypt.

Note the statue of Serapis in Room 6. This jolly looking god who combined the human look of Dionysios with the cult of the Apis bull was invented by the Ptolemies, in an effort to unite Greek and Egyptian culture. A giant statue of the Apis bull, found near Pompey's Pillar, stands in the centre of the same room. In Room 12 are sculpted heads of Alexander and Cleopatra.

The finest objects in the museum are the small Tanagra terracotta figures in Room 18A. They come from late 4th-century to early 2nd-century BC Alexandrian tombs of children, adolescents, and young women. Prompted by the sadness of death in youth, they are delicately expressive of life's moment.

Sharia Mathaf, north off Sharia Horreya. 1km east of Midan Sa'ad Zaghloul. Open: daily 9am–4pm. Closed: Fri 11.30am– 1.30pm. Admission charge.

Kom el Dikka

This area near the centre of Alexandria has revealed a Roman odeon (a theatre for musical performances) and a large complex of 3rd-century AD Roman baths. Excavation and restoration work is in progress. The site gives you an idea of how much of the ancient city could be recovered – if only the modern city were knocked down.

One of the great cities of antiquity, Alexandria is Egypt's largest port

Entrance on the south side of the large square, Midan el Gumhuriya, in front of the railway station. 1km southeast of Midan Sa'ad Zaghloul. Open: daily 9am–4pm. Closed: Fri 11.30am–1.30pm. Admission charge.

Kom el Shogafa Catacombs
The largest and weirdest tombs in Alexandria (*see p72*).
West off Sharia Amud el Sawari. 2.5km south of Midan Sa'ad Zaghloul. Open: daily 9am–4pm. Closed: Fri 11.30am– 1.30pm. Admission charge.

Nearby
Pompey's Pillar.

Montazah Palace and Gardens
Built in Turko-Florentine style at the end of the 19th century by the Khedive Abbas II, this was the royal summer residence. Notice the letter F used as a recurring motif outside. A fortune teller had told King Fuad that the letter would bring his family luck. So he and his son Farouk gave all their children names beginning with F.

Then, in 1951, Farouk married Narriman and neglected to change her name. In January 1952 she bore him a son, Ahmed Fuad, the F relegated to second place. Six months later King Farouk was out of a job.
16km northeast of Midan Sa'ad Zaghloul. Gardens open: 24 hours daily. Admission charge.

Pompey's Pillar
The Alexandrian acropolis once stood here (*see p72*).
Sharia Amud el Sawari. 2km south of Midan Sa'ad Zaghloul. Open: daily 9am–4pm. Closed: Fri 11.30am–1.30pm. Admission charge.

Qaytbay Fort
The fort stands on the site of the famous Ptolemaic lighthouse (*see p73*).
At the tip of the western arm of the Eastern Harbour. 3.5km northwest of Midan Sa'ad Zaghloul. Open: 9am–4pm. Closed: Fri 11.30am–1.30pm. Admission charge.

Ras el Tin Palace
See p73.
At the eastern tip of the Western Harbour. Closed to the public, but gardens are open. Admission charge.

Royal Jewellery Museum
Housed in the palace of an Egyptian princess, this collection covers the 150-year period from the rise of Mohammed Ali to the fall of King Farouk.
27 Sharia Ahmed Yehia, Glym. Open: daily 9am–4pm. Closed: Fri 11.30am–1.30pm. Admission charge.

Carriage Ride: Alexandria

Carriages, which can comfortably take two people, are the most delightful way to travel around Alexandria. Tell the driver where you wish to go.

By taxi, this tour will take you at least 3 hours.

Begin outside the Cecil Hotel on the Corniche at Midan Sa'ad Zaghloul.

1 The Cecil Hotel

This Moorish pile, built in 1929, is something of a landmark. Somerset Maugham, Noël Coward, and Lawrence Durrell have all signed its visitors' book. Take time to refresh yourself in its Art Deco tea lounge. Outside once stood the **Caesareum**, which Cleopatra built for Antony. There perhaps she committed suicide, and from there came Cleopatra's Needle, now in London, and the obelisk

Stanley Bay, along Alexandria's corniche

in New York's Central Park.

Head southwest to where Pompey's Pillar and Kom el Shogafa are close together.

2 Pompey's Pillar

Wrongly attributed by the Crusaders to the 1st-century BC Roman general Pompey, the pillar was raised at the end of the 3rd century AD to the emperor Diocletian. At its base are two pink granite sphinxes of the Ptolemaic period. This was once the city's acropolis, and here also stood the Temple of Serapis, a Graeco-Egyptian god invented by the Ptolemies. The temple was destroyed by a Christian mob in AD 391.

A short ride south is Kom el Shogafa.

3 Kom el Shogafa Catacombs

This largest Roman funerary complex in Egypt dates from the 2nd century AD. A winding staircase leads to an underground rotunda encircled by sarcophagi. Next to it is the banqueting hall where relatives of the deceased saw them out with a feast. At the level below is the central tomb chamber, decorated in a weird blend of classical and Egyptian styles. Inside stand dog-headed Anubis and crocodile-headed Sobek, both dressed as Roman centurions (*see p71*). *Head north to Midan el Tahrir.*

4 Midan el Tahrir to Fort Qaytbay

In the square is an equestrian statue of Mohammed Ali who brought Alexandria back to life in the 19th century. In Alexander's time, a causeway was built to the island of Pharos. Long ago silted up, its line is followed by Sharia Faransa running from the north-west corner of Midan el Tahrir through the picturesque old Egyptian quarter.

Towards the Western Harbour are the **Anfushi tombs** (*see p69*), while on the headland overlooking the harbour is **Ras el Tin Palace** (*see p71*). Here, on 26 July 1952, King Farouk abdicated and sailed into exile.

5 Qaytbay Fort

The present 15th-century fort was built by Sultan Qaytbay from fragments of the six-times taller Pharos lighthouse, which had been destroyed by earthquakes. Renowned as one of the seven wonders of the ancient world, the Pharos could, by means of a mirror, direct a beam of sunlight, or the light of a fire far out to sea (*see p71*).

6 Along the Corniche

Follow the Eastern Harbour back towards the Cecil Hotel, passing on your right the modern mosques of **Bouseiri** and, behind it, **Abu el Abbas** (*see p69*).

Excursions from Alexandria

The British War Cemetery, El Alamein

Abusir

The name Abusir contains, in trans-muted form, the memory of a small ancient city, Taposiris. Although the site is interesting and simple to get to, few people visit it as it is little known.

Taposiris stood at the western end of the same limestone ridge upon which Alexandria was built. Its ruins are slight, except for its tower and its temple. The enclosure walls of its **Temple of Osiris** are impressive, and there are pylons to climb for fine views over the delicate green marshes of Lake Maryut which lies to the south.

To the north the sea is astonishingly turquoise against the burning white coastal sand. The interior of the temple has disappeared, except for the foundations of an early church.

A few hundred metres to the east stands the tower, in fact a Roman lighthouse, built on the same pattern but one-tenth the size of the Pharos. *Along the Mediterranean coast road. 45km west of Alexandria, unprotected, always open and free. A hired car or taxi is needed to get here.*

El Alamein

The scene of the famous series of World War II battles is now marked by a museum with tanks and pieces of heavy artillery, while immediately to the east of the village is the starkly beautiful British Cemetery. The Italian and German cemeteries are respectively 8km and 12km further west.

On 17 July 1942, British General Auchinleck stopped Rommel's advance on Alexandria. Over the period 23 October to 5 November 1942, British Field Marshal Montgomery decisively defeated the Germans and put Rommel on the run. Within little more than six months the Germans and Italians were cleared from Africa altogether. *On the Mediterranean coast road. 106km west of Alexandria. Museum open: daily 9am–6pm, but closes at 3pm during Ramadan. Admission charge. Buses stop here between Alexandria and Mersa Matruh, but, although you can reserve a seat from Alexandria, you cannot at El Alamein, and will probably have to stand during the return journey. A hired car or taxi would be more practical.*

Mersa Matruh

While en route to the oasis of Siwa (*see p63*), you might wish to pause here for the magnificent beaches outside this one-time fishing port, now something of a boom town.

On the coast, 290km west of Alexandria. Service taxis and fast non-stop buses make the journey in 4 hours, while buses stopping at El Alamein and Sîdi Abd el Rahman take 5 hours.

Rashid (Rosetta)

Founded in the 9th century AD, Rosetta flourished as Alexandria declined. During the 17th and 18th centuries, it was Egypt's most important port. Many of its houses have been restored, and constitute the finest examples in Egypt of Islamic domestic architecture outside the capital, Cairo.

With the 19th-century refounding of Alexandria, Rosetta has in turn declined and is now a small agricultural market and fishing town, pleasantly situated on the western arm of the Nile, 10km from the sea. The town is most famously associated with the discovery here by one of Napoleon's soldiers of the **Rosetta Stone**, now in the British Museum. Because its inscription in ancient hieroglyphics is repeated in Greek, in 1821 Jean François Champollion succeeded in deciphering the ancient Egyptian language, thereby opening up Egypt's pharaonic past.

65km east of Alexandria. Both buses and service taxis make the trip.

Sîdi Abd el Rahman

This is a resort with a beautiful white beach. Accommodation is almost impossible to book during summer, but you might like to stop here for a swim when visiting El Alamein.

On the Mediterranean coast. 26km west of El Alamein, 132km west of Alexandria. Though buses and service taxis stop here, there is likely to be standing room only on the bus back to Alexandria.

Fishing boats off Rashid

East of the Nile

To travel east of the Nile is to enter another world. The level, green, and placid landscapes of Egypt's river and its Delta are left behind. Instead, mountains line the Red Sea coast, while central and southern Sinai are harsh and rocky, as though in a state of geological eruption. There is also the remarkable sight of the Suez Canal, the ceaseless passage of ships like patrols along a border.

The Greek Orthodox Church, St Catherine's

The impression of arriving at a frontier is due to a great rip in the earth's surface which extends from Africa's Rift Valley in the south to the valley of the River Jordan in the north. The **Red Sea** is extremely deep and its coastal mountains in the Sinai peninsula rise over 2,000m. Along with its northern finger, the **Gulf of Aqaba**, its enclosed waters are exceptionally warm and settled, encouraging the formation of coral reefs. The Gulf also attracts many brilliantly-coloured fish that make this one of the finest underwater panoramas in the world for adventurous scuba divers.

Sinai, too, offers adventure, not only along its coasts, but for off-road enthusiasts wishing to explore its vast sandscapes in the north, and the wild mountains and *wadis* of its central and southern interior. Tradition claims that Moses wandered among the jagged peaks in the south, an area of enormous historic significance, which accounts for the presence here of one of the most magnificent of all monasteries, that of St Catherine's, cradled at the foot of a dramatic outcrop of Mt Sinai (*see p80*).

El Arîsh

Until recently, El Arîsh was merely a Bedouin settlement on the Mediterranean coast of Sinai. Now it is the largest town on the peninsula with several hotels along its magnificent palm-fringed beach.
On Sinai's northern coast road. 278km northeast of Cairo via Ismailia and the Suez Canal ferry-crossing at Qantara. Alternatively, you can travel via the tunnel north of Suez, in which case the Cairo-El Arîsh distance totals 437km. There are also flights from Cairo.

Dahab

On the east coast of Sinai, and beautifully set against a backdrop of mountains, Dahab has two lifestyles; that of the fastidious tourist town to the south, and the ghetto-blasting, beach-bum scene 3km north on the edge of the pre-existing Bedouin village. But the great attraction is the reef fish. The tourist town offers the best diving shops and also the best reefs.
494km from Cairo via the Suez tunnel. The bus takes 8 hours. There are flights from Cairo to Sharm el Sheikh.

Feiran Oasis

The Feiran Oasis, the largest in Sinai, is like a secret garden of palms, tamarisks, and wheat set between towering mountain walls. Monks and hermits lived in the oasis during the early Christian centuries. Amid a plantation here, an avenue of column drums and capitals salvaged from ancient buildings leads up to a 19th-century chapel dedicated to Moses. Behind it are the ruins of a 4th-century bishop's palace.

South-central Sinai. 250km from the Suez tunnel en route to St Catherine's Monastery, and 395km east of Cairo (5½ hours by bus).

Hurghada

Once a fishing village, Hurghada is now a thriving, small city mainly dedicated to tourism. It has a variety of resort hotels only a few kilometres to the north and south of the city. These have clean, private beaches and are often totally self-sufficient. The town has an aquarium, but you should really hire a boat to the islands and reefs, where you can submerge yourself in the crystalline waters to enjoy a brilliantly coloured submarine world.

On the Red Sea coast road. 406km south of Suez, 550km southeast of Cairo (7 hours by bus), and 235km northeast of Luxor. Flights from Cairo and Luxor. An aquarium is on Sharia el Bahr. Open: daily 9am–10pm. Admission charge.

El Gouna

El Gouna is an attractive, new, purpose-built resort north of Hurghada on the Red Sea. It has a number of hotels and resorts to suit all pockets and is, in fact, a much more attractive place than Hurghada.

25km north of Hurghada and accessible by shuttle bus from Hurghada.

For off-road destinations in Sinai and the Red Sea mountains, see pp128–9; for more on the Red Sea resorts, see p142.

The sea off Hurgadha offers calm waters for sailing

Sharia el Gumhuriya, Port Said

Nuweiba

Less attractively situated than Dahab, and somewhat quieter, Nuweiba has a few diving facilities for exploring its fine reefs.
On the Gulf of Aqaba, on the eastern coast of Sinai. The distance from Cairo via the Suez tunnel is 560km. The bus takes 8½ hours. There are flights from Cairo to Sharm el Sheikh.

Ismailia

Midway along the Suez Canal, Ismailia is its operational headquarters. The town owes its character to the British, and its waterside district of wide, clean streets with suburban-style houses in well-planted gardens looks remarkably like a tropical England. The town museum exhibits recall ancient attempts to dig the canal. That job was finally accomplished in the 1860s under the direction of Ferdinand de Lesseps, whose house is on the main street as you come in from Cairo. On the canal there is a swimming club with a sandy beach, deck chairs, and refreshments, and hypnotic views of supertankers parading by.
128km northeast of Cairo, served by trains, buses, and service taxis. Museum open: daily 9am–4pm. Closed: Fri 11am–2pm. Admission charge. De Lesseps' House not generally open without permission from Suez Canal Authority.

Port Said

At the north end of the Suez Canal and with town beaches along the Mediterranean, Port Said prospered owing to its duty-free status. Along Sharia el Gumhuriya, two streets back from the canal, there are many beautiful old wooden buildings with balconies. The **National Museum** and the

MOSES AND THE EXODUS

How much, if any, of the story of the Exodus is historical is a matter of debate. Scholars accept that the Old Testament account was written by persons unknown, anything up to 1,000 years after the late second-millenium BC events described.

According to biblical tradition, Moses led the Children of Israel from Pi-Ramses in the Delta via the Red Sea, which obediently parted so they could walk across into Sinai. There, God gave Moses the Ten Commandments on top of a mountain, associated with Gebel Musa (Mount Sinai) near St Catherine's Monastery, which also claims possession of the Burning Bush. Moses made a Covenant with God atop Mount Sinai, promising him that the Israelites would obey the Ten Commandments. The Israelites wandered the Sinai for 40 years before finally entering the Promised Land.

small **Military Museum** are worth a visit, but the town's most famous landmark is the Suez Canal Building. Overlooking the canal itself, its gleaming white colonnade is crowned with three brilliant green domes. One way of getting a good view of the canal is to take the commuter ferry over to Port Fuad, a voyage from Africa to Asia.
200km northeast of Cairo, via Ismailia (4 hours). National Museum open: daily 9am–4pm; Closed: Fri 11am–1pm. Admission charge. Military Museum open: 9am–2pm, 7.30pm–8.30pm (10am–1pm Fri). Admission charge.

St Antony's Monastery (Deir Anba Antunius)

Surrounded by 2km of walls standing 12m high, St Antony's Monastery is dramatically set against the cliffs of the Eastern Desert plateau. St Antony, who died in AD 356, is the world's first historically documented Christian hermit, and the inspiration for the monastic movement. This monastery, founded by his disciples, claims to be the earliest in the world. Once rivalling the Greek Orthodox Monastery of St Catherine in beauty, it was sacked by Bedouins in the 15th century, but retains the parapets of the 10th-century walls, the 16th-century four-storey keep, and numerous frescoes of prophets and saints inside the 12th-century church. Against the south wall is the Spring of St Antony, while a two-kilometre path climbs up behind the monastery to St Antony's Cave.
On the Red Sea coast road, 120km south of Suez, follow the road inland for 30km before turning south for 10km to the monastery. There is no public transport. Accommodation available (see pp178–9).

The old grain mill, St Antony's Monastery

St Catherine's Monastery
(Deir Sant Katerin)

There are few more dramatic sights in Egypt than the tranquil Monastery of St Catherine lying against the flank of Mount Sinai. You approach from what is claimed to be the plain of Raha, where the wandering Israelites worshipped the golden calf, while above you looms the 2,285m mountain where Moses is said to have received the Ten Commandments from God.

Built in about AD 530, the monastery is Greek Orthodox, its monks mostly from Crete and Cyprus. Protected by its fortress-like walls, and respected by Jews, Christians, and Muslims alike for its associations with Moses, St Catherine's

Monastery has generally enjoyed the peace and patronage denied to Coptic monasteries, so that it preserves today all the splendour of its Byzantine past.

Outside its gate stands the Charnel House, heaped high with the bones of monks under the inattentive gaze of St Stephen the Porter, a 6th-century monk, dressed in a purple robe and holding a staff in his skeletal hand.

Dominating the interior of the monastery is the Church of the Transfiguration. Through the magnificently carved 6th-century inner doors of the narthex you enter the vast nave. At its far end is a gilded iconostasis adorned with large icons of John the Baptist, Mary, Jesus, and St Catherine, all 17th-century Cretan work. To the right, behind the iconostasis, is the reliquary which is said to contain St Catherine's skull and left hand. In the apse of the church is the 6th-century mosaic of the Transfiguration, one of the finest works of Byzantine art. Its subject is taken from *Matthew 17:1–3*. After Jesus had asked his disciples who they thought he was, he '. . . was transfigured before them: and his face did shine as the sun, and his raiment was white as the light.' On either side of the windows above the apse are mosaics of Moses taking off his sandals before the Burning Bush and receiving the Ten Commandments. Some of the monastery's 5,000 icons are displayed in the Icon Gallery next to the Library, which has a valuable collection of books and manuscripts, some dating to the 5th century AD.

A winding path climbs up Mount Sinai from behind the monastery. If you wish to have the mountain to yourself, wait until later in the day, but traditionally, visitors leave at 2am, allowing 2 hours for the climb, in order to reach the summit by sunrise. It can be cold, but the dawn is magnificent and the early morning light superb for photography. The walk is fine for any halfway fit person, and the route is easy to follow in the dark. As an alternative, you can hire a camel at the bottom. *In southern Sinai. 443km from Cairo. Buses take 6 hours. There are also flights and tours. Open: Mon–Thu & Sat 9am–noon. Closed: Fri, Sun & holidays. Free admission.*

Sharm el Sheikh, Na'ama Bay, and Ras Muhammad

Sharm el Sheikh and Na'ama Bay, 7km north, are twin resorts on Sinai's eastern coast. Sharm is popular with tourists, and together with Na'ama Bay is the bustling centre of activity. New resorts have sprung up along the coast to north and south with good accommodation and facilities for divers and non-divers.

The resort of Sharm el Sheikh

From Sharm you can take a boat to Ras Muhammad, a marine National Park at the southernmost tip of Sinai, where there are superb views across the Gulf of Suez to the Red Sea mountains and across the Gulf of Aqaba to Saudi Arabia. But most spectacular are its underwater views, though the sea can be rough out at the reefs, where diving is not really suitable for beginners. Everyone, however, can enjoy the underwater snorkelling. *514km southeast from Cairo. Buses, stopping at Sharm and Na'ama Bay, take 6 hours. There are flights to Sharm from Cairo and Hurghada, and a ferry sails between Sharm and Hurghada. There is no public transport to Ras Muhammad other than boat trips from Sharm. Admission charge.*

Suez

Badly affected by the 1967 and 1973 wars with Israel and the sporadic shelling in between, Suez is now a largely rebuilt industrial centre. The Ahmed Hamdi Tunnel, 12km north, is the main route for traffic into Sinai. *134km east of Cairo, reached by trains, buses, and service taxis.*

The idea of a canal to link the Red Sea with the Mediterranean is by no means a modern conception. The earliest historically authenticated attempt was made by Necho, a 26th-Dynasty pharaoh, who abandoned the project when an oracle warned that only the Persians would benefit from it. Indeed it was the Persian King Darius I who completed it a century later, in about 500 BC.

The first canal ran from the Red Sea to about where present-day Ismailia stands, before turning westwards to Bubastis, near modern Zagazig, to join up with a now vanished arm of the Nile. It was maintained by the Ptolemies and the Romans, but was abandoned by the Arabs.

The present canal, at 167km, is the third longest in the world, and the longest without locks. Its completion in 1869, under the direction of the Frenchman Ferdinand de Lesseps, was a great feat for Egypt and of major importance to world trade. That narrow strip of land saved shipping from the States and Canada, Britain and Europe having to travel the length of Africa, cutting thousands of miles off their journey. It opened up trade to parts of the world previously restricted, and brought invaluable revenue to Egypt.

Nasser's nationalisation of the foreign-owned Suez Canal Company in 1956 was a reaction to nearly a century of direct or indirect Western rule. This led to the Suez Crisis, an attack on Egypt by Britain, France, and Israel, called off after Soviet and American objections. It was one of the most tense and dangerous moments of the Cold War. The 1967 war with Israel closed the canal for eight years, and the shelling of the canal towns during that time caused enormous damage.

In 1975 President Sadat reopened the canal. As many as 50 ships pass through every 24 hours with an average transit time of 15 hours. They carry with them a significant amount of the world's trade, and the fees they pay are a major income-earner for Egypt. A new bridge links East and West, making the crossing from mainland Egypt to Sinai easier.

The Suez Canal – one of the world's most vital passages for trade

The Nile Valley

Cairo to Luxor

Throughout Egyptian history a distinction has been made between Lower Egypt, which is the land of the Delta, and Upper Egypt, where the desert and mountains encroach upon the Nile Valley with its narrow band of cultivation. Lower Egypt, then and now, has been more cosmopolitan, more exposed to foreign influences. From Upper Egypt have come periodic bursts of conservative reaction.

Ancient Memphis and now Cairo stand near the juncture of the Delta and the Nile Valley, but the sense of entering Upper Egypt only really begins when you have got beyond Beni Suef, a busy and unattractive town 124km south of Cairo. From this point, you are leaving behind those most impressive monuments of the Old Kingdom at Gîza and Saqqâra. The Nile Valley is more associated with later pharaonic periods, though along this first stretch of the river, heavily populated by Copts, there are also several interesting early Christian sites.

Abydos

Ancient Abydos was the shrine of Osiris, who as god of the underworld, was also a central figure in the Egyptians' notions of resurrection and the afterlife. The 19th-Dynasty New Kingdom pharaoh Seti I, though possessing a mortuary temple in the Theban necropolis, built one here as well. Reacting against Akhenaton's revolution in worship and art *(see box)*, Seti was

Relief carving on entrance pillar

OSIRIS AND ATON

The cult of Osiris formed part of the orthodox religion of ancient Egypt. The story goes that Osiris, son of Re, was a king who ruled justly and was greatly loved in distant times. Isis was his sister and wife, and Seth was his brother. When Seth killed Osiris and dismembered his body, Isis searched out the pieces and put them together again. Abydos, where Isis found Osiris' head, became a national shrine. Just as she restored him to life in the underworld, so all who followed the Osiris cult would share in the promise of resurrection and eternal life.

The 18th-Dynasty pharaoh Akhenaton rejected both the priesthood of Amun at Thebes and the Osiris cult, and was called a heretic. At Amarna, he worshipped instead the Aton, the solar disc, to whom he wrote a hymn, which is found in many of the Amarna tombs.

determined to reinstate Egyptian style as it had existed during the Old Kingdom.

The first hypostyle hall was decorated after Seti's death by his son, Ramses II. The more finely carved and coloured work on the walls of the second hypostyle hall (some of the finest reliefs to be seen anywhere in Egypt) were executed during Seti's lifetime. They include profiles of Seti himself, which closely resemble the distinctive features of his mummy at the Museum of Egyptian Antiquities in Cairo (*see p40*).

At the left of the second hypostyle hall is a passageway known as the Gallery of the Kings for its cartouches of Seti's

predecessors back to the time of Menes. This has proved invaluable to Egyptologists in determining the correct order of pharaonic succession. Adjacent reliefs show Seti himself and his son, the future Ramses II, revering their ancestors.

600km south of Cairo, on the west bank of the Nile. 10km southwest of El Balyana, which is 40km northwest of Nag Hammâdi. Several Cairo–Luxor trains stop at El Balyana, from where service taxis run out to Abydos. Alternatively, take a tour or hire a taxi from Luxor, visiting both Abydos and Dendera. These are also covered by some cruises. Open: 7am–5pm. Admission charge.

Atmospheric Abydos, sacred to the memory of Osiris, the god of resurrection

Asyût

With a population exceeding 260,000, Asyût is the largest town in Upper Egypt. Home to an Islamic university, Asyût has long been a centre for fundamentalist activity. There have been sporadic outbursts of violence against the security forces and against tourists, and a strong military presence is maintained. Now it is relatively peaceful. *378km south of Cairo. Buses depart from here for the oases of the Western Desert.*

Beni Hasan

A path leads up from the east bank of the Nile to 39 Middle Kingdom tombs cut into the cliff face, though only four are normally open to the public. These tombs belonged to provincial governors and are exceptional for the detail of their paintings which depict agriculture, craft, hunting, and sports, along with occasional military scenes, giving a vivid impression of everyday life.
On the east bank of the Nile. 275km south of Cairo and 25km south of El Minya. A taxi from El Minya will take you to the ferry landing; on your return it can take you on to Amarna. Open: 8am–5pm. Admission charge.

Dendera

For the ancient Egyptians, the goddess of joy and love was Hathor, the cow goddess, whose name means Castle of Horus. As a fertility goddess she suckled Horus, the son of Isis and Osiris, and then lay with him at Edfu. Each year a

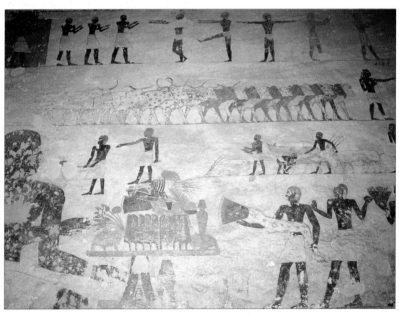

Detailed wall paintings at Beni Hasan throw light on everyday life in Egypt

Monumental gateway to Dendera

great pageant takes place at her temple at Dendera culminating in this event.

Every dynasty legitimised itself by identifying with various aspects of the Osiris story, and the Ptolemies were no exception. This **Temple of Hathor** at Dendera is their construction, and later, even the Romans took a hand, adding the pylon-shaped façade with its six Hathor-headed columns.

You pass through a succession of halls which become smaller, lower, and darker, until you reach the inner sanctuary of the goddess. Normally kept bolted and in darkness, it was opened and illuminated by torchlight to allow Hathor's adoration by the pharaoh. This ritual is depicted on wall reliefs inside.

At the New Year, images of the goddess were carried up to the roof where they made contact with the rays of Re – a spiritual emergence from darkness into light. You can retrace the route by climbing the stairways from within the temple, their walls incised with reliefs illustrating the procession. Near the base of the west stairway is the New Year Chapel. On its ceiling is a magnificent relief of Nut, the sky goddess, giving birth to the sun whose rays illuminate Hathor. On the roof is the elegant kiosk where Hathor was exposed to the sun's revivifying force, while above the stairwells are the twin chapels of Osiris, their decorations including a zodiac (though the original has been removed to the Louvre, Paris). Colossal reliefs on the outside rear wall of the temple show Caesarion, son of Julius Caesar, with his mother, the great Cleopatra, and last of the Ptolemies.

618km south of Cairo, on the west bank of the Nile. 4km west of Qena. From the train station you can take a taxi or carriage to the temple. Alternatively, take a tour or hire a taxi from Luxor, visiting both Dendera and Abydos, which are also sometimes covered by cruises. Temple open: 7am–6pm. Admission charge.

El Minya

Within easy reach of Beni Hasan and Amarna, El Minya, which has a large Christian community, has unfortunately taken over from Asyût as a centre for unrest, and suffers from sporadic outbursts of violence. Nevertheless, its warm and friendly population enjoys promenading along its winding riverside corniche, while amid overgrown gardens stand charming villas, once the homes of Greek and Egyptian cotton magnates. *On the west bank of the Nile. 250km south of Cairo.*

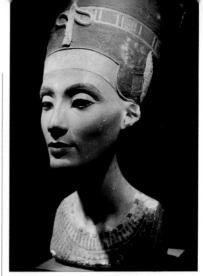

Original bust of Queen Nefertiti

MONASTERIES ALONG THE NILE
Burnt Monastery (Deir el Muharraq)

Unusually, this flourishing Coptic monastery is not far off in the desert but just within the cultivated zone. By tradition this marks the southernmost point in the flight of the Holy Family. Here, it is said, Joseph heard the angel's words as recorded in St Matthew's Gospel: 'Arise, and take the young child and his mother, and go into the land of Israel.' A church dating back at least to the 8th century and dedicated to the Virgin, El Adra, stands over the cave where the Holy Family supposedly stayed. Next to it is a 12th-century keep. Annually, during the week of 21 June, more than 50,000 people collect here to attend the Feast of the Consecration of the Church of the Virgin.

On the west bank of the Nile. About 30km south of the ferry crossing for Amarna, 80km south of El Minya, and 40km north of Asyût. A taxi tour could be included in a tour of Beni Hasan and Amarna. For details on Coptic monasteries, see pp178–9.

White Monastery (Deir el Abyad)

As you follow the road out from Sohâg you see a startling sight. At the edge of the cultivation, with its back against the hills of the desert plateau, stands what seems to be an intact Egyptian temple. This is known as the White Monastery, and is the most remarkable instance of the similarity between Coptic and pharaonic architecture.

Massive white limestone walls slope inwards and are finished off with a cavetto cornice of white marble. Inside is an enormous basilical church. To call it a monastery is misleading, for the ruins of that once vast structure housing over 2,000 monks now lie beneath the mounds of rubble outside. The surviving building is in fact a fortified monastery church built in about AD 440 by St Shenute, whose *moulid* is celebrated here during the week leading up to 14 July.

The nave is in ruins – much of the damage was caused by Mamelukes fleeing Napoleon's troops in 1798. Nevertheless, the proportions of the church, both the exterior and interior, and the broken columns of marble and black granite make a noble impression. What was the sanctuary has been bricked off to form a complete church, its apses arranged as a trefoil, with 12th-century paintings adorning their semidomes.

Sohâg is 470km south of Cairo. From there a taxi can take you the 5km west to the White Monastery. Open: daily 7am–6pm; all night during the moulid. Free admission.

Tell el Amarna

When the 18th-Dynasty pharaoh Akhenaton broke with the worship of Amun at Thebes in favour of the sun disc Aton (*see p84*), he founded his new capital Akhetaton ('Resting Place of the Disc') at the place now called Tell el Amarna, or simply, Amarna. The city was abandoned after the deaths of Akhenaton and his beautiful queen Nefertiti. Thebes once again became the capital, and a compliant Tutankhamun was persuaded to reinstate the worship of Amun.

Only the merest traces of palaces, temples, and houses remain in this great sand-filled crescent between the Nile and the cliffs of the Eastern Desert. The cliff-face tombs offer a splendid view back over the plain.

There is a lonely and melancholy beauty to Amarna, but for its paintings, reliefs, and sculptures you must visit the Museum of Egyptian Antiquities in Cairo (*see p40*).

On the east bank of the Nile. 314km south of Cairo and 67km south of El Minya. From El Minya, take a taxi to the west bank ferry landing and cross over to the village of El Till. The site lies behind the village. Access is unrestricted and free. At the village you can hire donkeys or a tractor to visit the tombs, 4km east. Open: 7am–5pm. Admission charge.

A dusty track to the Tell el Amarna rock tombs is well worth the climb

The River of Life

Journeying through Egypt by road or rail, you miss the grandeur of the Nile. It is only by air that you get a bird's eye view of the mighty river, and the strip of cultivation to either side. However, when you sail for days along the Nile there is the clear sense that you are travelling along a valley, seeing sights that have not changed since time immemorial, a mixture of ancient and modern, biblical and secular.

In the early stages of the journey from Cairo to Aswân, the Nile cuts through rock and cliffs close on either side. These then fall away into the distance, and only fields can be seen, villages and vegetation, and people going about their daily life, washing their clothes and pots and pans in the river, children swimming, and animals cooling down in the water.

Agriculture is very important to the economy of Egypt. Crops of all sorts are grown in the fertile Delta and along the cultivated strips either side of the Nile. There is sugar cane, maize, and *barseem*, the clover fed to animals. Rice is grown, as are a variety of fruits and vegetables. Date palms proliferate, ranging from nearly black to pale yellow, either hard or soft, sweet or tart. Mango plantations and citrus groves are everywhere. At all times, one is reminded of how the river has forced its way through the arid desert and carved its passage through rock bringing life to its banks. Life is also brought to the people of Egypt as a result of the trade on the Nile. Barges plough up and down the river, carrying their cargoes of stone and other valuable commodities which are cheaper to transport by river. *Feluccas (see pp132–3)* also ply their trade, not only in tourist towns and cities, but also as a means of transport from one side of the river to the other.

The pharaohs regarded the river with reverence, and their myths and beliefs are all inter-related. The Nile is indeed the artery of Egypt – a living, working river – the lifeline of the country today as it was in the past.

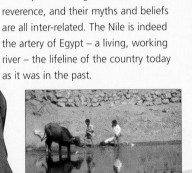

The Nile, Africa's longest river, is the most picturesque record of Egyptian daily life

Luxor

The name Luxor is loosely applied by travellers to include three distinct places: the town of Luxor, with a population over 150,000, on the east bank of the Nile; the village of Karnak and its immense temple 4km north on the same bank; and the Theban necropolis on the west bank of the river opposite Luxor and Karnak. At the height of its glory during the 18th and 19th Dynasties, Thebes covered all of what is now Luxor and Karnak, and may have had a population as high as one million. Earlier, in Middle Kingdom times, its most important god had been Amun. When the Theban princes drove the alien Hyksos out of Lower Egypt and reunited the country, Thebes became capital of the New Kingdom, and Amun became Egypt's national god.

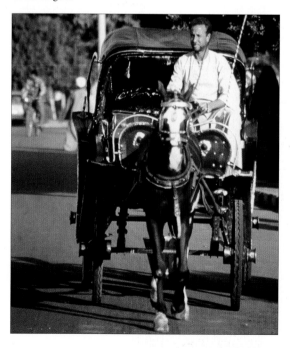

VISITING THE WEST BANK

As soon as you arrive at the west bank of the Nile buy tickets for the tombs and temples of the Theban necropolis that you want to visit that day. Generally, you will only be allowed to visit three tombs in the Valley of the Kings. Some are likely to be closed. Keep alternative choices in mind. You will not be allowed into the sites wihout a ticket and these are only valid on the day of issue. Tickets for Tutankhamun's tomb can only be purchased at the security gate entrance to the Valley of the Kings.

The ticket office is open from 6am. It is just up the road from the Colossi of Memnon statues for which you do not need a ticket. Tombs and temples are open 6am–6pm. All charge an admission fee. The west bank can be reached by taxi or tour bus by crossing Luxor Bridge, 8km south of the city centre. The ferry is not always available.

Luxor and Thebes

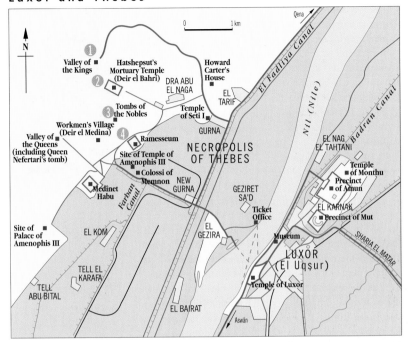

Apart from its military prowess, Thebes was also strategically situated between the agriculturally rich Delta and gold-rich Nubia. It is tempting to believe that the great pharaohs of the New Kingdom also responded to the beauty and never-failing fertility of the surrounding landscape.

It did inspire them to build, sometimes sensitively, sometimes grandiosely, and Thebes became the focus of an architectural activity so magnificent, and still well enough preserved, that it can lay just claim to being the world's greatest outdoor museum.

On the east bank, highlights include the Temple of Karnak, scene of the Sound and Light show, and the Luxor Temple (and Museum), which includes the Mosque of Haggag. The west bank highlights (in numbers on map) are covered by a taxi tour of the Theban necropolis (*see pp106–7*) which includes the Valley of the Kings, the Valley of the Queens, Hatshepsut's mortuary temple, and the Colossi of Memnon.

Obelisk at the entrance to the Temple of Amun at Karnak

Colossi of Memnon

The mortuary temple of Amenophis III has vanished, and all that remains are the two famous colossi which once guarded its outer gates. They are, in fact, gigantic statues of the enthroned Amenophis himself, 19.5m high. At one time they wore the royal crown and were even higher.

The one on the right (north) was shattered by an earthquake in 27 BC and later repaired; for nearly 200 years thereafter it would often emit a musical note as the sun rose over the eastern mountains. Greek and Roman tourists, including the emperor Hadrian in AD 130, camped overnight to witness the unusual phenomenon, and carved their names into the colossi's legs.

On the west bank in the southern part of the necropolis. 3.5km from the Nile.

Hatshepsut's Mortuary Temple (Deir el Bahri)

Hatshepsut's father, the 18th-Dynasty pharaoh Tuthmosis I, was the first to seek greater security for his mummified body by having a tomb dug in the Valley of the Kings. Hatshepsut followed his example, and ceremonies in her honour were held at her mortuary temple (*see p107*) built directly over her tomb chamber where she is thought to be buried. Early Christians used it as a monastery, which is why it is often known as Deir el Bahri, the Northern Monastery.

The temple has three terraces linked by ramps. The Lower Terrace was a garden with myrrh trees and fountains, as though a foretaste of that life which endures even in the other world. Within the right colonnade at the rear of the terrace this theme is continued in delicate reliefs depicting an idealised country life. At the rear of the Middle Terrace, reliefs to the left, along the Punt Colonnade, show Egyptians who had sailed south along the African coast to obtain myrrh trees for the temple being greeted by the chief of Punt and his extraordinarily corpulent wife. Reliefs along the Birth Colonnade to the right announce Hatshepsut's divine parentage. Her father as Amun sits opposite her mother Ahmosis, who is then led to the birth chamber.

'WONDERFUL THINGS!'

About his discovery of Tutankhamun's tomb, Howard Carter wrote: 'Details of the room within emerged slowly from the mist, strange animals, statues, and gold – everywhere the glint of gold. For the moment – an eternity it must have seemed to the others standing by – I was struck dumb with amazement, and when Lord Carnarvon, unable to stand the suspense any longer, enquired anxiously "Can you see anything?" it was all I could do to get out the words, "Yes, wonderful things".'

As a woman pharaoh, Hatshepsut was eager to underline the legitimacy of her rule, especially as it was being challenged by her stepson and nominal co-ruler, the future Tuthmosis III. When he finally came to the throne, following her death, he resentfully defaced her images here on the pillars of the Birth Colonnade and elsewhere, while preserving his own. The Upper Terrace, now restored, is still closed.

On the west bank, at the north end of the necropolis. 6km from the river. See box on p92 for ticket details.

Howard Carter's House (Qasr Carter)

On a barren hill overlooking the road which rises towards the Valley of the Kings is the large domed house where the archaeologist and artist Howard Carter lived during the time of his discovery of Tutankhamun's tomb. He had earlier worked for the Egyptian Exploration Fund, recording scenes from the walls of tombs and temples.

At the north end of the necropolis. 1km north of Seti I's mortuary temple and 5km from the river. Closed to the public.

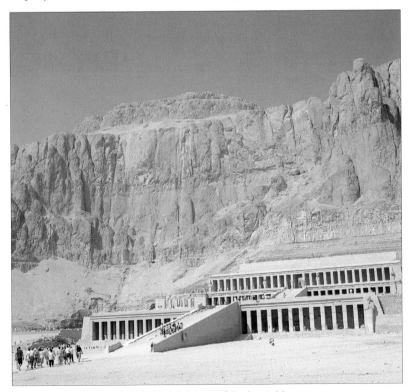

Hatshepsut's Mortuary Temple (Deir el Bahri) rises out of the desert plain

Karnak

The Karnak site covers a huge area. The precinct of Amun in fact encloses several temples, but most people will be content to walk through the biggest of these, the Temple of Amun, the gigantic proportions of which are immensely larger than both St Paul's Cathedral in London and St Peter's Church in Rome.

One dynasty after another added to the Temple of Amun so that, from its founding during the Middle Kingdom to the building of its outermost or First Pylon during the 25th Dynasty, 1,300 years elapsed. The Asian conquests of Tuthmosis III and Ramses II brought New Kingdom Egypt to the peak of power and prosperity. The great god Amun also received his share, so that his temple soon controlled perhaps as much as a fifth of Egypt's workforce and owned nearly a third of its land.

Something of this story is told during the Sound and Light show which leads you briskly through part of the **Temple of Amun**, and deposits you in the grand-stand over-looking the Sacred Lake.

By day you will have more of a chance to get your bearings. A processional way lined with ram-headed sphinxes leads into the temple. They represent Amun, and between the forelegs of each is a diminutive figure of the god's servant, Ramses II. The First Pylon was built 600 years later. At 43m high it is the largest at Karnak, and nearly twice the size of the entrance pylon at the Temple of Luxor. A succession of pylons funnel you towards the sanctuary of the god.

Passing through the Second Pylon you enter the Hypostyle Hall, the 19th-Dynasty work of Seti I and Ramses II. Its forest of columns is one of the most spectacular sights in Egypt. Each column is so massive that it takes the outstretched arms of six people to encircle one. Originally, the entire hall was roofed over. An obelisk

SOUND AND LIGHT

On the east bank. 4km north of Luxor. Open: daily 6am–6pm in summer; 5pm in winter. Admission charge. Sound and Light shows are held daily, with three or four performances during the course of the evening. They tell the story of Thebes, and some of the pharaohs, and at least one show per night is in English. The others alternate between French, German, Italian, Spanish, Japanese, and Arabic. Admission charge.

raised by Tuthmosis I stands in the small court between the Third and Fourth Pylons. Between the Fourth and Fifth Pylons stood two magnificent obelisks of Tuthmosis I's daughter, Hatshepsut. One has snapped in half; the upper portion lies at the northwest corner of the Sacred Lake where you can examine its fine hieroglyphic inscriptions. The other remains in place, and at 29.5m is the tallest obelisk in Egypt. You will notice two pink granite pillars carved with lilies on one side and papyrus flowers on the other, the traditional symbols of Upper and Lower Egypt. Past these is the Sanctuary of the Sacred Boats, built in the time of Alexander the Great to replace the original. Along the south flank of the Temple of Amun is the Sacred Lake where the god's sacred boats took part in various ceremonies, culminating in the annual Opet festival when he sailed upriver to the Temple of Luxor. At its northwest corner, by part of Hatshepsut's obelisk, is a gigantic scarab dedicated to the rising sun.

The overpowering hypostyle hall of the Temple of Amun, with its gigantic columns

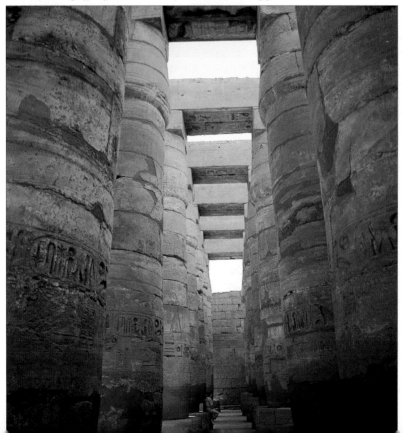

Luxor Museum

The museum contains a small but carefully selected number of beautifully displayed exhibits. Graeco-Roman, Coptic, and Islamic artefacts are included, but the overwhelming emphasis is on the pharaonic period.

There are a few items from Tutankhamun's tomb, including a funerary bed, model boats, and a golden cow's head. The other contents of his tomb are all in the Museum of Egyptian Antiquities in Cairo. Reliefs of Akhenaton and Nefertiti worshipping Aton, and scenes of their palace life are also displayed.

Most outstanding, however, are the black basalt and pink granite statues and busts of jug-eared Sesostris III of the 12th Dynasty, and of the 18th-Dynasty pharaohs Tuthmosis III, Amenophis II, and Amenophis III. The craftsmanship is superb, and you can feel the sculptors' enjoyment of working with the graceful curves of crowns, necks, and waists.
On the east bank, on Sharia Nahr el Nil. 1km north of the Temple of Luxor. Tel: (209) 380269. Open: daily 9am–1pm & 5–9pm in winter; 9am–1pm & 5–10pm in summer. Admission charge.

Luxor Temple

Until the end of the 19th century, when excavations began, almost the whole of Luxor village stood within and on top of this debris-filled temple. Only the mosque of Abu Haggag was allowed to remain perched on top of its walls.

Gilded cow's head, Luxor Museum

Unlike Karnak, which was built over a long period of time, the Temple of Luxor is largely the work of the 18th-Dynasty pharaoh Amenophis III. With him began the fashion for gigantism that broadcasts the imperial pretensions of New Kingdom Egypt.

It was Ramses II, however, who later built the entrance pylons and the great court beyond. In front of the pylons he placed six colossal statues of himself, only three of which remain. Of the two obelisks he erected here, one was given to the French by Mohammed Ali and now stands in the Place de la Concorde in Paris. Incised on the pylons are scenes of the battle of Kadesh in Syria, which Ramses claimed as a victory against the Hittites, though he was lucky to escape from it with his life. The vertical grooves on the pylons were made in order to support flagstaffs.

Numerous colossi of Ramses stand around the great court, his wife Nefertari knee-high at his side. On the far right-hand wall a relief shows the exterior of the temple, complete with colossi and obelisks, and banners waving from the pylons. From here, you enter the imposing colonnade of Amenophis III. On the right-hand wall are reliefs dating from the reign of Tutankhamun depicting the Opet festival, an annual fertility rite during which Amun sailed from Karnak for a conjugal reunion with his wife Mut, who resided at the Temple of Luxor with their son Khonsu.

The Court of Amenophis leads to his Hypostyle Hall with interesting reliefs on its far walls showing his coronation by the gods.

These in turn lead on to the Sanctuary of the Sacred Boat of Amun, corresponding to the one at Karnak. Its inner chamber was rebuilt during the time of Alexander the Great. On the outside wall facing the river is a relief of a pharaonic-looking Alexander offering gifts to Amun who is in a state of presumably festive erection.

Returning back through the temple and emerging again at the pylons, you notice the avenue of sphinxes that once led all the way to Karnak.

On the east bank, on Sharia Nahr el Nil at the centre of Luxor. Open: daily 6am–10pm, 9pm in winter. Admission charge. After dark, the temple is beautifully floodlit, creating a dramatic effect.

Putting Ramses II at Luxor Temple into perspective

Medînet Habu
(Mortuary Temple of Ramses III)

Ramses III's great mortuary temple is usually known as Medînet Habu, 'town of Habu'. During the Coptic period there was a town of some size, while part of the temple was used as a church.

Modelled closely on the Ramesseum, which had been built less than a century earlier, the temple of Ramses III is much better preserved, and is second in size only to the Temple of Amun at Karnak. It was, however, to prove the last major architectural work of the pharaonic period, as during the rest of the 20th Dynasty, Egypt's fortunes declined. You enter the site by a gatehouse which, judging from the reliefs on the walls of its upper storey, served as a resort where the pharaoh could amuse himself with the harem women. Straight ahead is the First Pylon which is worth climbing to gain an overall impression of temple layout, the pylons, columns, and chambers becoming smaller and smaller as you gaze towards the sanctuary.

This was not only a mortuary temple, but also a royal residence. The First Court was the scene of ceremonies and entertainments, the pharaoh perhaps making appearances at the window in the left-hand wall which was also the palace façade. During the Ptolemaic and Roman periods, the Second Court was filled with houses and a church – the octagonal base of its font can be seen on the left. Beyond this are three hypostyle halls leading to the sanctuary which once contained Amun's boat. Left off the Second Hypostyle Hall is the funerary chamber of Ramses III with depictions of Thoth inscribing the pharaoh's name.

Painting and relief carving in the Temple of Seti I and Ramses II at Abydos

If you now go back through the First Pylon and turn left, you can walk round to the outside wall of the temple to see its famous panoramic relief. This shows the attempted invasion of Egypt by the Sea Peoples, a coalition of northerners who had already overrun the Hittite empire in Anatolia (present-day Turkey) and Syria. They are shown arriving in ships and overland by ox-cart, bringing their families and all their belongings, attacking the Delta, and being repulsed by Ramses himself.

An inscription graphically describes the outcome: 'A net was prepared for them to ensnare them, those who entered into the rivermouths being confined and fallen within it, pinioned in their places, butchered and their corpses hacked up.'

On the west bank, at the southern end of the necropolis. 5km from the river.

Nobles' Tombs

Hundreds of nobles' tombs have been found in the Theban necropolis. Two of the most interesting, those of Ramose and Sennufer, are described on page 107. Also worth visiting, if you have the time, are the tombs of Rekhmire, Menna, Nakht, Userhat, and Khaemhat. *On the west bank near, and sometimes under, the village of Sheikh Abd el Gurna. 5km from the river. They are signposted from the Ramesseum.*

The Ramesseum
See p107.
On the west bank, at the centre of the Theban necropolis. 5km from the river.

Seti I's Mortuary Temple
If you are unable to see Seti's exquisite reliefs at Abydos (*see opposite & pp84–5*), then you should visit his temple here. Some of the reliefs are best seen from above, so you leap goat-like after the resident guide, from lintel to broken lintel.
On the west bank, at the north end of the Theban necropolis en route to the Valley of the Kings. 4km from the river.

Ticket Details
See box on p92 for ticket details.

Relief carving in the Temple of Ramses II, Luxor

Valley of the Kings

Leaving the cultivated zone behind, the road climbs towards the Valley of the Kings, an oven of white sand and sun containing 62 tombs, almost all belonging to pharaohs of the 18th, 19th, and 20th Dynasties (1570–1090 BC). The tombs were cut into the soft limestone by workmen living at Deir el Medina. Construction and decoration began as soon as a pharaoh came to the throne, and followed a similar pattern in all the tombs. Three corridors lead to an antechamber giving on to a main hall with a sunken floor for receiving the sarcophagus.

The Valley of the Kings is 7km west of the Nile, along a steeply rising road which curves round the Theban necropolis. The hardy can leave the area by a mountain track starting between Tombs 10 and 16. It divides at the top of the ridge, the left arm descending to Hatshepsut's mortuary temple, the other going on to Deir el Medina.

The recurrent theme of the decorations has the dead pharaoh, absorbed in the sun god, sailing through the underworld at night in a boat, with enemies and dangers to be avoided along the way. Inscriptions from the *Book of the Dead* provide instructions for charting the course. After this nocturnal voyage the naked body of the sky goddess Nut gives birth each morning to the sun.

It is thought the dramatic discovery of Tutankhamun's tomb in 1922 was the last, and that all the tombs have now been found. Most are of little interest except to scholars and are therefore closed to the public.

Only tombs 2, 6, 8, 9, 11, 16, 17, 34, 35, 57, and 62 have electric lighting, (which, in any case, is not very bright), and not all of these are always open. Most visitors will be content to see the tombs of Tutankhamun (62), Ramses VI (9), Seti I (17), and Ramses IV (2). Even some of these, unfortunately, may be closed when you visit.

Tomb 2: Ramses IV (20th Dynasty)

The New Kingdom was already in decline when this tomb was cut. Its decorations are of inferior quality, but the patterns of bright colours against an overall background of white, and the excellent lighting, contribute towards a favourable impression.

There is much Ptolemaic and Coptic graffiti throughout, particularly to the right of the entrance where two haloed saints raise their arms in prayer. The ceiling of the sarcophagus chamber is decorated with the goddess Nut.

The huge pink granite sarcophagus is covered with texts and magical scenes, while Nephthys and Isis on the lid were meant to protect the body – which was, nevertheless, hijacked in antiquity and never found.

Tomb 9: Ramses VI (20th Dynasty)

Originally constructed for Ramses V, this tomb ended after three corridors, but was later extended for Ramses VI, to double its length. The colouring remains fresh throughout. The pillared end-chamber contains fragments of the huge granite sarcophagus. A magnificent painting of Nut in duplicate adorns its low vaulted ceiling.

Tomb 17: Seti I (19th Dynasty)

At 100m, the Tomb of Seti I is the longest in the valley. Its reliefs are wonderfully preserved and beautifully executed. On the left wall of the entrance corridor, Seti is greeted by falcon-headed Re-Herakhte, god of the morning sun. The next two corridors are decorated with instructions from the *Book of the Dead* on how to navigate the underworld.

In the three chambers beyond, Seti is shown with various deities. These motifs are then repeated in the second half of the tomb. Finally, there is the burial chamber with astronomical figures on the vaulted ceiling. In the small chamber to the right, the sky goddess Nut is shown in the form of a cow.

Tomb 62: Tutankhamun (18th Dynasty)

This tomb is described on page 106.

Valley of the Kings

VALLEY OF THE QUEENS

This valley contains over 70 tombs of queens, princes, and princesses of the 18th, 19th, and 20th Dynasties, although only four are open. Unlike the pharaohs, however, these lesser royal figures were not gods, and so their tombs are more humble affairs.

Tomb 66: Queen Nefertari (19th Dynasty)

Nefertari was the wife of Ramses II, and is celebrated in stone at Abu Simbel and elsewhere. Her tomb, long closed owing to damage caused by salt deposits, has been marvellously restored and reopened. It is by far the finest in the valley, the wall paintings exquisitely drawn and vividly coloured. Admission is restricted to 150 people a day, so it is better to get to the ticket office early to avoid disappointment, and there is a premium admission charge.

Tomb 55: Prince Amun-Her-Khopshef (20th Dynasty)

A smallpox epidemic towards the end of Ramses III's reign killed off several of his sons. In the hall at the bottom of the entrance steps there is a painting showing the pharaoh introducing one of them, Amun-Her-Khopshef, to the gods. The paintings throughout this tomb are fresh and finely executed. At the centre of the burial chamber there is a sarcophagus in human, or rather, mummy form.

The bones of a six-month-old foetus are displayed in a glass case, and for this very reason, rather than the clarity of the paintings, this tomb seems to hold the attention longer.

Tomb 44: Prince Khaemweset (20th Dynasty)

Belonging to another son of Ramses III who fell victim to smallpox, the decorations of this tomb are similar to those of Tomb 55, and are more easily observed, as there is no foetus here to draw the crowds.

Tomb 52: Queen Titi (20th Dynasty)

Although inscriptions describe Titi as a daughter, wife, and mother of pharaohs, it is not known to which pharaohs these refer. The paintings are badly faded and damaged. The tomb is arranged like a cross, a corridor leading to a central and three smaller chambers. In the small chamber on the right, Titi is shown with a tree-goddess, and Hathor as a cow. She also appears on the left and right walls of the small chamber ahead.

WORKMEN'S VILLAGE (Deir el Medina)

Deir el Medina means 'monastery of the town', for the workmen's village and the small Ptolemaic temple just north of it were occupied by monks during the early years of Christianity. During the New Kingdom, this was home to skilled artisans who cut and decorated the royal tombs in the Valley of the Kings.

The remains of over 70 houses are evident, their mud-brick walls rising on stone foundations along straight and narrow alleys. They had a second storey, or at least a living area on the roof, reached by outside stairs. They also fashioned their own tombs, but unlike those of the nobles who decorated their tombs with vivid scenes of everyday life, these workmen more often borrowed motifs from the Valley of the Kings. Over the tomb entrance they would build a man-sized pyramid.

Usually only two or three of these tombs are open. The tomb of Sennedjem (Tomb 1) has a vaulted chamber down steep steps, in which there is a finely painted relief of a funeral feast, and also a nice cameo touch of a cat killing a snake under the sacred tree. The tomb

of Peshedu (Tomb 3) shows him praying beneath the tree of regeneration.

On the west bank at the southern end of the Theban necropolis, 4.5km from the river. See p92 for ticket details.

The Valley of the Queens is on the west bank, at the southern end of the Theban necropolis, 5km from the river. (*See p92 for ticket details.*)

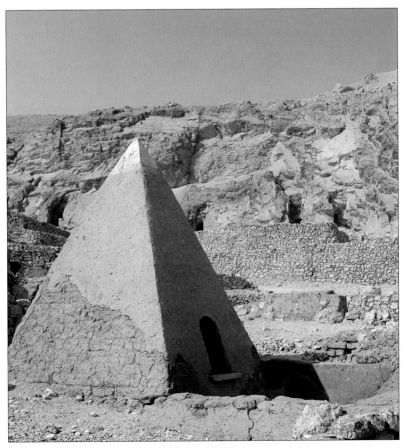

One of the many man-sized pyramid tombs at Deir el Medina

Tour: The Theban Necropolis by Taxi

Allow 4 hours to complete this highlight tour of the necropolis. See page 93 for a map of the tour.

Begin at the west bank ticket office. Drive across the cultivation and up through the desert hills into the Valley of the Kings.

Mask of Tutankhamun

1 Tutankhamun's Tomb

Discovered by Howard Carter in 1922, this is the only tomb in the Valley of the Kings to have been found with its contents intact. Owing to the pharaoh's early death at 19 (he had ascended to the throne at the age of 12), the tomb is small and was hurriedly decorated. Its treasures have been removed to Cairo. All that remains here now is the open sarcophagus. Within it lies the outermost of the three gold sarcophagi, and, unseen within that, the mummy of Tutankhamun himself. The right wall shows the coffin transported on a sled. The centre wall shows, from right to left, the opening of the mouth ceremony, Tutankhamun sacrificing to the sky goddess Nut, and the young pharaoh with his *ka* before Osiris. On the left wall is the sun god's boat. The Tomb of Seti I should also be visited. For details of this and other tombs in the Valley of the Kings, see pages 102–3.

Arrange for your driver to meet you at Deir el Bahri while you walk (or take a donkey) over the path rising out of the Valley of the Kings between tombs 10 and 16. At the top of the ridge, turn left, then descend to Hatshepsut's temple.

2 Hatshepsut's Mortuary Temple (Deir el Bahri)

Apart from Cleopatra, Hatshepsut was the only woman to rule as pharaoh, and she immortalised her reign by brilliantly setting her temple against a pyramid-shaped cliff face to create a powerful yet elegant ensemble (*see pp94–5*).
Immediately south is the village of Sheikh Abd el Gurna, built upon a hillside dotted with nobles' tombs.

3 Tombs of the Nobles

Unlike those in the Valley of the Kings, the nobles' tombs are more intimate. Others are listed on page 101.

Sennufer's Tomb

This 18th-Dynasty mayor of Thebes was probably also chief vintner to Amenophis II, and you wonder whether his tomb is not his last laugh on that theme. Vines and grapes are painted on wobbly ceilings, walls, and pillars, as though you and Sennufer had had one drink too many.

Ramose's Tomb

Ramose was vizier to Amenophis IV, and as you follow these exquisitely carved reliefs around the walls you witness one of the great revolutions in Egyptian history. Begun in classical style, the reliefs continue in the Amarna style, because Amenophis IV had decided to become Akhenaton, and thereafter changed the art and religion of his country.
South from the village is the Ramesseum.

4 Ramesseum

This huge mortuary temple of Ramses II is such a confusing ruin that it is more than sufficient to look at his gigantic fallen statue. Into its mouth Shelley put these ironic words from his poem *Ozymandias*: 'Look on my works, ye Mighty, and despair!'

Alternatively, or additionally, visit Medînet Habu (allowing 30 minutes). Its temple of Ramses III is more complete than the Ramesseum.

Driving south from the Ramesseum and then east, you can pause at the Colossi of Memnon (*see p94*) before continuing over the bridge and back to the east bank.

Fallen head of Ramses II

The Nile Valley

Luxor to Aswân

The Valley of the Nile narrows south of Luxor and the desert impinges more closely on either side. The ribbon of cultivation seems more fragile, its colours more delicate, and the debt that life in Egypt owes to the river becomes more striking. You notice this especially on the east bank beyond Edfu where a narrow strip of palms and cultivation sometimes vanishes altogether.

Like a string of citadels extending Alexandrian power towards Nubia, the Ptolemies built temples along the Nile at Esna, Edfu, and Kom Ombo. At Silsileh, 40km south of Edfu, the Nile passes through a defile. Now there are only hills on either side, but there was probably once a cataract. The bedrock of Egypt changes here from limestone to the harder sandstone used in almost all New Kingdom and Ptolemaic temple building. During the reign of Ramses II, the Silsileh quarries were worked by no fewer than 3,000 men for the Ramesseum alone.

Statue of the god Horus

Edfu

The present town of Edfu, on the west bank of the Nile (*see p137*), is spread upon the mound of the ancient city of Djeba, which the Ptolemies – who identified the Greek sun god Apollo with Horus – called Apollinopolis Magna. Here, according to myth, Horus avenged the murder of his father Osiris by defeating Seth in titanic combat. To mark this triumph of good over evil,

a succession of shrines was built here from earliest dynastic times, culminating with what is the best preserved ancient monument in Egypt, the Ptolemaic Temple of Horus on the west side of the town.
115km south of Luxor.

Temple of Horus

Until the latter part of the 19th century the temple was almost entirely covered by debris, and houses stood upon its roof. Only its enormous pylon rose clear above the habitations. Even today, the surrounding town obscures your view of it from any distance. And so the impression is all the greater when you arrive at the site and suddenly see the temple all at once. Its enormity is striking, and its near-perfect state of preservation makes it seem like a recent leftover from some epic Hollywood spectacular.

Construction began in 237 BC and continued for 25 years, though some of the decorations were not completed for another 150 years after that. Despite his New Kingdom appearance, the giant pharaoh shown destroying his enemies on the pylon façade is Ptolemy XII Neos Dionysos, who died in 51 BC. He built also at Dendera and was the father of Cleopatra. You pass across a vast colonnaded courtyard towards a pair of huge granite falcon-Horuses, one standing, the other headless and fallen in the dust, which guard the entrance to the temple chambers. These chambers become ever smaller, ever darker, and lead finally to the sanctuary of the god, weirdly illuminated through three small apertures in the ceiling by a dim green light. The reliefs on the inner walls of the sanctuary correspond to those at Dendera, and show a Ptolemaic king entering the sanctuary and worshipping Horus, Hathor, and the king's own deified parents. His pendant arms indicate an attitude of reverence.

A sensuously-shaped relief of Nut decorates the ceiling of the New Year Chapel which is to the left as you emerge from the sanctuary. Nearby, staircases lead up to the roof, with representations along their walls showing, as at Dendera, how the residing deity was carried up to the roof to be impregnated by the sun.
Western outskirts of Edfu, 2km from the Nile. A carriage can be hired at the quayside. You can walk in 20 minutes from the service taxi depot near the bridge or the train station on the east bank of the river, though private taxis are available from either. Open: daily 6am–6pm in summer; 7am–4pm in winter. Admission charge.

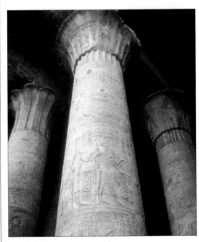

Pillars inside the Temple of Horus

Esna

Like other towns along the Nile, Esna was, until the end of the 19th century, a port of call for camel caravans crossing the desert from the Sudan (*see p137*). It is still something of a merchant town and weaving centre, with elegant old houses along the west bank of the Nile and in the streets behind. Several of these houses are decorated with fine brickwork and *mashrabiyya* screens. There is also a small and picturesque covered market street, where lengths of fabric are sold or made up into clothing.

Temple of Khnum

Only partly excavated, the Temple of Khnum squats in a pit alongside the covered market street. Here you still have some impression of how many of the ancient monuments appeared until Egyptologists went to work on them in the 19th century, for the rear of the temple remains buried beneath a mound of debris which is partly built over with houses.

Ram-headed Khnum was the patron god of the Cataracts who fashioned man from the mud on his potter's wheel. Ptolemy VI rebuilt the temple in the

Baubles, bangles, and beads

One of the many falcon statues at the temple

mid-second century BC over the ruins of earlier structures, although almost all that the excavators have laid bare is the hypostyle hall begun two centuries later during the reign of the Roman emperor Claudius.

The roof of the hall is still intact, supported by 24 columns bearing painted capitals in 16 different styles. This is what you come to see, and it is best to stand here, slowly revolving, looking upwards at the myriad palm and composite plant capitals, arranged without order or symmetry, but with the most pleasing effect, as though you were standing among trees, admiring the subtle and powerful architecture of a forest. The last cartouche carved on the temple walls is that of the Roman emperor Decius, who reigned from

AD 249 to 251. He began a series of increasingly severe persecutions against the new Christian religion, and decreed that all its followers must sacrifice to the Roman gods or suffer death.

Testimony to his lack of success in Egypt is to be found in the forecourt of the temple where there are several blocks from an early Christian church, including a lion-headed font carved from an ancient block bearing fine hieroglyphics on the reverse.

Esna is 55km south of Luxor. The Temple of Khnum is at the centre of Esna, a few streets west of the Nile landing stage. It is a 10-minute walk from the service taxi depot; carriages are available from the more distant train station. Open: summer, daily 6am–6.30pm; winter, daily 6am–5.30pm. Admission charge.

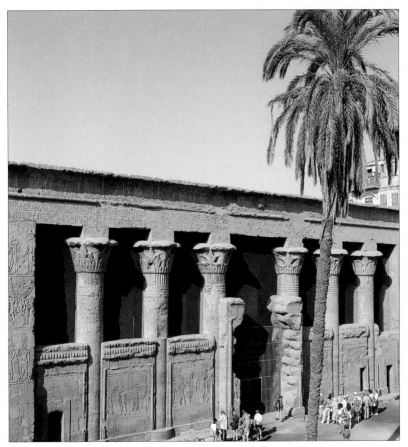

The hypostyle hall of the Temple of Khnum

Kom Ombo

The reclaimed land on the east bank around Kom Ombo supports a large Nubian population displaced from their homeland by the rising waters of Lake Nasser. Irrigation keeps the desert at bay, and the fields give rich harvests of wheat and sugar cane. A few kilometres away from the village with its sugar refinery is the Ptolemaic temple.
170km south of Luxor, 45km north of Aswân.

Temple of Sobek and Haroeris

The temple stands on a low promontory overlooking the Nile. Its elevation, its seclusion, and the river flowing by below, make it a magical place to visit, especially from a *felucca* or cruise boat. Its relationship to the landscape reminds you of a Greek temple but, though built by Greeks and added to by Romans, the style is pharaonic. As with all Ptolemaic temples, the intention was to reconcile the Egyptian priesthood to foreign rule from Alexandria.

The naos or inner temple was begun by Ptolemy VI Philometor, who built also at Esna, while the hypostyle hall and the pronaos were built by Ptolemy XII Neos Dionysos, whose reliefs adorn the pylon at Edfu. The outer court and the now vanished pylon

were added during the time of Emperor Augustus.

This is a symmetrical twin temple, the left side dedicated to falcon-headed Haroeris (Horus in his older aspect), the right side to Sobek, the crocodile god. The two parts of the temple are only physically divided, however, at the two sanctuaries.

You enter the site past a giant ruined gateway, and near it, a small chapel of Hathor. If you wander into the chapel you can see that it is now used as a display room for crocodile mummies dug up from a cemetery close by. The Nile has nibbled away at the temple terrace, causing the pylon to fall, and so you walk directly into the pronaos, its column capitals – some as lilies, some as papyrus – proclaiming the unity of Upper and Lower Egypt. On the interior wall of the façade are fine reliefs depicting various Ptolemaic kings receiving the blessings of Egypt's high gods, and the double crown of the Delta and the Nile Valley.

In the hypostyle hall beyond, and in the three rising antechambers after that, are more reliefs. One, between the doors into the two sanctuaries, shows Ptolemy

Painted pillar at the Temple of Sobek and Haroeris (Horus)

The temple at Kom Ombo, dedicated to Sobek (the crocodile god) and Haroeris (Horus)

Philometor and his sister-wife before Sobek and Haroeris, while Khonsu, son of Amun, inscribes the king's name on a palm stalk, the equivalent of St Peter confirming entry into heaven.

The sanctuaries are badly ruined, but they are all the more revealing for that. Between them, at a lower level, is a crypt which communicates with a chapel to the east. The crypt is now exposed, but was once covered with a sliding slab. It is not difficult and somewhat eerie to imagine someone creeping down there from the chapel to make spectral noises at appropriate moments.

An inner corridor passes behind the sanctuaries, and is lined by chapels in various stages of decoration. Beyond this there is an outer corridor, its walls decorated with Roman reliefs. If you face away from the sanctuaries and look just to the left of centre you will see a relief of the Roman emperor Marcus Aurelius, famous among other things as a Stoic philosopher, but here made to look for all the world like a New Kingdom pharaoh.

To his left are fascinating reliefs of medical instruments, including suction cups, scalpels, retractors, scales, lances, bone saws, chisels for surgery within the skull, and dental tools – testimony to the remarkable degree of medical sophistication in Egypt nearly 2,000 years ago.

4km from Kom Ombo village, with its train station and service taxi depot. Cruise boats, however, tie up directly below the temple. Open: daily 8am–8pm. Admission charge.

R u r a l   L i f e

Until the building of the High Dam at Aswân during the 1960s, the Nile annually rose and fell, inundating the surrounding countryside and then withdrawing, leaving behind a rich deposit of mud. There are still some remnants of Egypt's flood-led lifestyle. Villages of mud-brick houses still stand huddled on the low mounds which once kept them clear of the murky waters. Age-old devices continue to be used to bring water to the fields. The simplest and most ancient of all is the *shaduf*, a bucket attached to a lever, operated by hand. The *sakiya*, introduced in Ptolemaic times, consists of a number of buckets attached to a wheel driven by a circling donkey or ox. Also Ptolemaic is Archimedes' screw, a spiral enclosed within an inclined cylinder which raises water when it is turned.

But the ancient pattern of rural life is changing rapidly. The annual deposits of mud have been replaced by chemical fertilisers, produced by factories operating on the hydro-electric power generated by the High Dam. Harvests have multiplied, but the fields and the river offer fewer nutrients now, and the numbers of birds and fish are diminishing. Even the mud itself has

The *fellahin*, Egypt's peasantry, depend on farming for their livelihood, and agriculture remains the basis of the country's economy

now become an unrenewable resource, and concrete is increasingly being used instead of mud-brick when building houses.

Electricity, however, has brought light to the villages at night – and television, too. The *fellahin*, Egypt's peasantry, are no longer isolated from the wider world. Electric and petrol-driven pumps are replacing the dulling labour of men and animals. Education and primary health care have improved. This ought to have brought brighter prospects. Instead, improved health care has brought a population explosion. *Fellahin* seeking a better existence have been abandoning their diminishing plots in the desperate hope of a better life in the cities, which now hold half of Egypt's population. Food and jobs are short. The rhythm of the past has been broken, and the future is perilous.

Aswân

The layer of sandstone covering Upper Egypt from Edfu southwards is ruptured here by the thrust of underlying granite which the river has sculpted into the rocks and islands of the First Cataract. Throughout history, this is where traffic on the Nile stopped, where cargoes had to be transported round the rocks. Aswân became the entrepôt for the African trade. The sands finally close in upon the river here, and there is no more buffer of cultivation on either side. The air is hot, but also wonderfully dry, accounting for Aswân's fame as a winter resort. Although there are things to see, the town's tranquil atmosphere and the beauty of its situation is more conducive to idleness. Fortunately, idleness and sightseeing can be combined by hiring a *felucca* and letting the breeze carry you along.

Elephantine is the long palm-covered island opposite Aswân. There is a ferry to the Nubian villages. Otherwise you can hire a *felucca* to reach the island's antiquities.

Aga Khan's Mausoleum
See pp134–5.
On the west bank of the Nile, but closed to the public.

Botanical Garden
See p134.
This botanical island garden, known also as Kitchener's Island, lies between Elephantine Island and the west bank of the Nile and is reached by felucca. *Open: daily 8am–sunset. Admission charge.*

Dier Anba Samaan
(St Simeon's Monastery)
See p135.
On the west bank of the Nile, 2km from the river. From the landing stage, you can walk across the sands in about 20 minutes, or hire a camel. Open: daily

9am–5pm (4pm in winter).
Admission charge.

Nubian Museum
This delightful modern museum is dedicated to the history and culture of Nubia, and well worth a visit. All the artefacts were found in Nubia, and include a head of King Taharqa, the first Nubian to rule Egypt, and exhibits representing contemporary Nubia.
Tel: (209) 319111. Open daily 9am–1.30pm & 6–10pm (winter 5–9pm).

Elephantine Island
In ancient times the area on the east bank of the Nile, where Aswân now stands, was known as Syene and was famous for the nearby quarries of pink granite. Yet it was always secondary to

Yebu, in the south. Yebu was Egyptian for elephant; while Elephantine was the later Greek name, reflecting its important ivory trade.

Aswân Museum

Very little now remains here as most of the artefacts have been moved to the Nubian Museum, but it is worth a look. *Open: Sun–Thu 8am–5pm (6pm in summer), Fri 9am–1pm. The admission ticket is valid also for Yebu ruins.*

Nilometer

This shaft cut down into the granite bluff on the east side of the island is inscribed with pharaonic, Greek, Latin, and Arabic numerals. It was used for measuring the height of the Nile – and therefore the likely harvest, and the tax to be imposed on farmers (*see p38*). *A path from the museum runs 300m southeastwards towards a sycamore tree, where you will find the Nilometer. Open: as Aswân Museum. Baksheesh to keeper.*

Yebu

Excavations here have revealed the remains of several temples, and also the remains of the homes of the Jewish garrison posted here during the 5th century BC. *Entry to the museum includes admission to the ruins.*

Elephantine Island, in the middle of the Nile, sits opposite the modern town of Aswân

The High Dam Circuit

It is usual, when visiting the High Dam, to stop – or at least glance at – a few other places of interest along the way. Altogether, the circuit south from Aswân to the unfinished obelisk, then over the old Aswân Dam and back to the east bank via the High Dam, is about 18km. Taking a tour or hiring a taxi is the easiest option. Photography at the dams is not permitted, and it is a good idea to bring your passport for identification.

A camel rests at the site of ruins near Aswân

Old Aswân Dam

Built between 1898 and 1902, this dam was part of a vast hydrological project undertaken by the British up and down the length of the Nile, which included barrages at Esna, Nag Hammâdi, and just downriver from Cairo. The height of this dam was twice raised to increase irrigation and hydro-electric output. A

The unfinished obelisk measures over 27m

road passes over the top of the dam and looks down upon the First Cataract below, though it hardly swirls now.

Aswân High Dam

As the population continued to grow, the old dam could no longer meet Egypt's need for new cultivatable land and increased supplies of electricity. Work began on the High Dam, 6km upstream, in the mid-1960s, and was completed in 1971. Seventeen times as much material went into its construction as was used to build the Great Pyramid of Cheops, and enough metal to build 17 Eiffel Towers. A huge artifical lake, Lake Nasser, reaches back 500km to the Second Cataract in the Sudan. Were the dam to break, a tidal wave would rush down the Nile Valley, inundating most of Egypt's rural and urban population.

Although there are environmental drawbacks, there are also undeniable advantages. The British dam regulated the flow of the Nile during the course of a year; the High Dam can store surplus water over a number of years, balancing

The Nile near the Aswân Dam

low floods against high, and ensuring up to three harvests a year. It has already proved its worth. During the 1980s the Nile fell to its lowest levels in 350 years, bringing drought and famine to Ethiopia and the Sudan, but Egypt was spared, and millions of lives saved.

A road passes over the dam, and towards its eastern end there is a viewing platform where you can gain some feeling for the size and controlled energy of the place.

The High Dam can be crossed from 7am to 5pm. There is a toll per person.

Unfinished Obelisk

The favoured pink granite found in ancient monuments throughout Egypt and even beyond came from Aswân, much of it from the quarry where you can still see an unfinished obelisk rooted to the bedrock. The work was undertaken during the New Kingdom, and had it been completed, it would have been the largest piece of stone

handled in history. Work stopped after a flaw was discovered in the stone.

The ancient quarry is 2km south of Aswân. Open: daily 6am–6pm. Admission charge.

Kalabsha Temple

Rebuilt here in the 1970s, this temple's original site was 50km south, in that part of Nubia now beneath the waters of Lake Nasser. It dates from the time of Augustus, and the emperor is shown making offerings to the Egyptian pantheon, for which, in real life, he had the greatest contempt.

At the western end of the High Dam. Open: daily 8am–4pm. Admission charge.

Nobles' Tombs

See p134.

The tombs are on the west bank, and can be reached by ferry from the northern end of the Aswân corniche, or by felucca. Open: daily 8am–5pm. Admission charge.

Philae

Completion of the British dam in 1902 submerged the island of Philae for half the year, so that visitors needed to row out upon the river to look at the tops of the temple pylons and columns. In fact, a sense of romance and mystery grew up around the experience. Construction of the High Dam made things worse, however, leaving Philae permanently and almost entirely drowned, so the temples of this historic site were moved.

The decision was taken to transfer the monuments from the old island to another, called Agilqiyyah, which has been moulded to replicate the original. The present site was opened in 1980, and with the growth of vegetation it is impossible to guess that the temples have not been standing here for 2,000 years. Apart from the Vestibule of Nectanebos I, a pharaoh of the 30th Dynasty, the Philae monuments are Ptolemaic and Roman. There are minor temples to Harendotes and Augustus. The three principal monuments, however, are the Kiosk of Trajan, the Temple of Hathor, and the Temple of Isis.

Kiosk of Trajan
On the south side of the island stands this handsome but unfinished building, with 14 great columns bearing beautifully carved floral capitals. Reliefs show Trajan offering incense and wine to Isis, Osiris, and Horus. The elegance of the kiosk has made it the characteristic symbol of Philae.

THE CULT OF ISIS

Isis, as wife of Osiris and mother of Horus, increasingly became the focus of worship. The goddess offered an emotive identification so powerful and satisfying that in Ptolemaic times she became identified with all other goddesses of the Mediterranean world, whom she finally absorbed. Isis was the Goddess of Ten Thousand Names. When all else failed, she could still save, and she was passionately worshipped by all. She was the great rival of early Christianity, which may never have given the Virgin Mary prominence but for the Isis cult.

PHILAE

Philae, just south of the old Aswân dam, can be reached by taxi and motorboat from Aswân. The island is open daily 7am–6pm. Admission charge. There are nightly **Sound and Light** shows. Check for language schedules first.

Philae

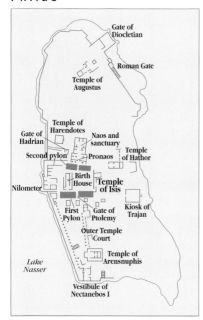

often accompanied by merry-making.
The Greeks identified her with the
goddess of love, Aphrodite.

Temple of Isis

Two great pylons lead into the temple
proper. They are carved with the
traditional scenes of Ptolemaic kings,
attacking the enemy on the First Pylon,
on the Second Pylon making offerings
to Isis, Horus, and Hathor. The walls of
the pronaos are likewise covered with
scenes of Ptolemaic kings and Roman
emperors in pharaonic guise,
performing the customary ceremonies.

Later, when this became a church,
early Christians added their crosses to
the stones. The three antechambers of
the naos lead through to the sanctuary
with a pedestal on which stood the
sacred boat with the image of Isis. On
the left wall is a relief of a pharaoh
facing Isis whose wings protectively
embrace Osiris. On the right wall, Isis
enthroned suckles the infant Horus,
while below that she is shown again,
suckling a young pharaoh. Here her face
was gouged out by Christians.

Temple of Hathor

On the east side of the island, this
temple was built during the Ptolemaic
period, but decorated under Augustus
with amusing carvings of music and
drinking, for the worship of Hathor was

The Temple of Isis (below) and the
Temple of Hathor (left) were moved
to a new site because of flooding

Walk: The Aswân Corniche and Bazaar

This walk is less a matter of seeing sights than of sensing the spirit of the place. It is best to begin an hour or so before sunset.

Allow 2 hours. You may want to linger along the way.

Begin on the Corniche el Nil, opposite the northern tip of Elephantine Island, and walk southwards. Follow the numbers shown in green on the map.

1 Corniche el Nil

There is a special fascination in the vista as you walk along the Corniche at Aswân. Instead of the usual placid cultivation, a tidal wave of desert rises on the far bank, islands force the Nile into channels, and boulders break the river's surface like gigantic bathing pachyderms. Although ugly concrete buildings line the landward side of the street, and a hotel looking more like an airport control tower disfigures the northern tip of Elephantine Island, the

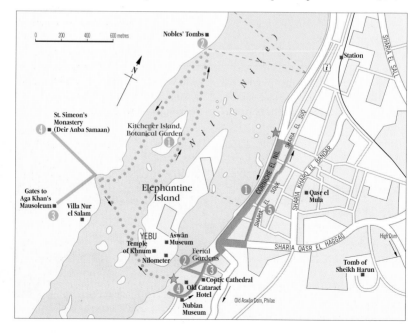

elemental beauty of the setting remains. The shrine of a Muslim holy man sits on top of the bare hill on the west bank of the Nile, beyond the northern point of Elephantine. The row of small dark openings in the flank of the hill marks the ancient tombs of Aswân's nobles.

Towards the centre of Elephantine Island are Nubian villages, the houses painted pale yellow or brilliant blue. *The road now turns away from the Nile and begins to climb a hill.*

2 Ferial Gardens

On your right, between the road and the Nile, are the Ferial Gardens, standing upon great loaves of granite overlooking the river. Opposite, at the southern tip of Elephantine Island, you can make out the remains of the ancient town of Yebu (*see p116*).
Across the road from the gardens is a Coptic cathedral.

3 Coptic Cathedral

Built in 1900 to resemble a domed Coptic church, this was, in fact, the Anglican Church of St Mark, its font a gift of Queen Victoria of England. It has now become a Coptic cathedral, to which visitors are welcome.
Continue south along the road. About 300m on, you arrive, on your right, at the entrance way to the Old Cataract Hotel.

4 Old Cataract Hotel

The exterior of this 1902 russet pile featured in the film of Agatha Christie's *Death on the Nile.* If you have timed your walk well, you will have arrived here half an hour or so before sunset. The hotel has a terrace from where,

drink in hand, you can enjoy wonderful views over the Nile. However, please note that sometimes non-residents may not be able to enter the hotel. (*See Aswân, p172.*)
When finally the sky has gone through deepening violets to black, set off back down the hill as far as the Ferial Gardens. Instead of going along the Corniche, however, turn right into Sharia Qasr el Haggag, and then take the first left into Sharia el Souk.

5 Sharia el Souk

This is the main bazaar street of Aswân, the best bazaar outside Cairo. Sensibly, in a place which is so burning hot during the day, it is only now, when the sun has set, that it becomes thronged with people.

The first 500m of Sharia el Souk retains something of the atmosphere of the old caravan days. Spices, gum, and ebony out of Africa are traded here, alongside locally woven rugs and other goods. Buy yourself some freshly baked flat bread along the way, and wash it down with pressed cane juice.

Souvenirs in Aswân's bazaar

Excursion from Aswân

Abu Simbel

Two temples stare out from the cliff face at Abu Simbel. On the left is the Temple of Re-Herakhte with its colossi of Ramses II, and on the right the smaller Temple of Hathor, associated with Ramses' queen, Nefertari. Before the creation of Lake Nasser, the temples overlooked a bend in the Nile and dominated the landscape. As statements of Egyptian might, they served as a warning to any troublesome Nubians, while offering a welcome to peaceful traders arriving out of Africa.

Entrance to the pink sandstone temple of Queen Nefertari, wife of Ramses II

Temple of Hathor

The façade is in the form of a buttressed pylon. Between the buttresses are six colossal statues of Ramses and Nefertari. Heads of Hathor adorn the columns of the hypostyle hall inside. On the entrance wall are reliefs of Ramses slaying his enemies, and a very graceful Nefertari with her arms upraised in prayer. Beyond this is the sanctuary with Hathor, as the divine cow, emerging from the rock wall. This, and the façade, suggest the overall symbolism of the temple, which complements that of Re-Herakhte's.

There, Ramses identifies himself with Horus-as-sun-god; here, Nefertari is identified with Hathor, who was wet-nurse and mistress to Horus, as well as wife to the sun god during his day's passage, and mother to his rebirth.

So, in the temple, Hathor emerges as though from the world beyond, where her milk brings life to the souls of the dead; while Nefertari emerges with Ramses into the morning sun.

ABU SIMBEL

It is 280km south of Aswân, and can be reached by road. There are also flights from Aswân, Luxor, and Cairo, a hydrofoil service once a day, and the MS *Prince Abbas* cruises between Lake Nasser and Aswân (*see p162*). Open: 6am–5pm. Admission charge includes local guide.

RESCUING THE TEMPLES

Construction of the Aswân High Dam during the 1960s would have meant the drowning of the Abu Simbel temples beneath Lake Nasser. Instead, the UNESCO operation raised them to a new and higher site nearby. As the original temples had been cut into a giant cliff face, an artifical mound had to be constructed, and the temples set into it. A small doorway to the right of Re-Herakhte's temple lets you inside the now air-conditioned dome area.

Temple of Re-Herakhte

Arranged in pairs on either side of the entrance are the four enthroned colossi of Ramses, taller than the Colossi of Memnon at Thebes, wearing the double crown of Upper and Lower Egypt.

Osiris-type figures of Ramses stand against the piers of the hypostyle hall within. The battle of Kadesh, in which the Egyptians were nearly defeated by the Hittites, is depicted on the left, and Ramses is shown appealing to Amun. On the right, a triumphant Ramses is shown storming a Syrian fortress and capturing Hittites. In the next hall of four pillars Ramses and Nefertari are shown before the boats of Amun and Re-Herakhte. Beyond is the sanctuary, where a divinised Ramses sits with Ptah, Amun, and Re-Herakhte. The temple progressively depicts Ramses, therefore, as conqueror, hero, and then god.

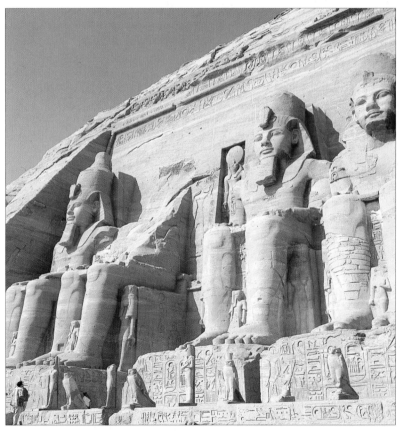

The 20-m high colossal figures at the Temple of Ramses II at Abu Simbel

'If you go to Thebes', Josephine is reported to have said to Napoleon, 'do send me a little obelisk.' The imperial capitals of Rome and Constantinople had long ago acquired Egyptian obelisks; and though the British drove Napoleon from Egypt before he could satisfy Josephine's desire, Mohammed Ali made good the growing appetite for Egyptian antiquities by presenting obelisks to Paris, London, and New York.

That appetite was stimulated by Napoleon's invasion in 1798, when the scholars accompanying him compiled the famous *Description de l'Egypt*, the first systematic study of the country, both ancient and modern. It was also during the French occupation that the Rosetta Stone was discovered. Using its parallel Greek text as a key to its ancient Egyptian text, Champollion succeeded in deciphering hieroglyphics in the early 1820s (*see p28*). Now it was possible to read the ancient Egyptians' own descriptions of their lives, their accomplishments, and their beliefs.

Scholars such as the Frenchman Auguste Mariette, the German Richard Lepsius, and the Englishman Sir Flinders Petrie laid the foundations for modern Egyptology. Nevertheless, throughout the 19th century, the recovery of information remained secondary to the acquisition of objects. Scholars and adventurers alike freely exported almost anything they discovered – now part of the great collections at the British Museum, the Louvre, and elsewhere.

In 1922 all that changed with the discovery of Tutankhamun's tomb by Howard Carter and Lord Carnarvon. The spectacular find awakened the interest of an increasingly nationalist Egypt in its ancient heritage. The old rule of finders-keepers was challenged, and instead of being taken abroad, the treasures were put on display in Cairo. The modern

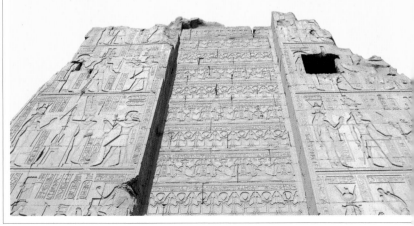

spirit is expressed by the UNESCO inscription at Abu Simbel: 'These monuments do not belong solely to the countries who hold them in trust. The whole world has the right to see them endure'.

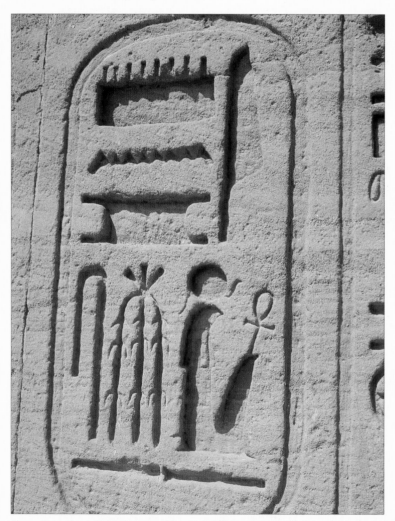

Above: Cartouche enclosing the name of Ramses II at his temple in Abu Simbel
Facing page: Symbols and stone reliefs of kings on the temple at Kom Ombo

Desert Driving and Camel Trekking

'Perhaps the most wonderful part of desert life is the desert night', wrote the Egyptian explorer Ahmed Hassanein early this century. 'It is as though a man were deeply in love with a very fascinating but cruel woman. She treats him badly, and the world crumples in his hand; at night she smiles on him and the whole world is paradise.'

'The noses, ears, mouths and eyes of our party carried away enough of Egypt, which had been held suspended in the air, to found an oasis in the desert.'

WILLIAM JARVIE
Letters Home from Egypt and Palestine, 1903–4,
New York, 1904

Paradise can in fact be approached by public transport, which follows paved roads to all the oases of the Western Desert. Hiring a vehicle, however, with or without a driver, will give you greater freedom to explore.

Some roads in remote areas, such as those between the oases of Baharîya and Farafra, and particularly between Farafra and Dakhla, can get badly potholed and sandswept, but provided your car has been well maintained, a two-wheel drive vehicle should be

entirely adequate for on-road driving anywhere in Egypt. Take sensible precautions, such as taking plenty of water and petrol, travelling in pairs in remoter areas, and avoiding night driving over dodgy roads.

Off the Beaten Track
As soon as you get off the road, however, even just to camp overnight in the desert, you must have a four-wheel drive vehicle. Fortunately, you can sleep out beneath the stars in the must-see

The White Desert

White Desert, 50km north of Farafra. White chalk formations are nightly licked into abstract sculptures by the windblown sand, and everything, both desert and sleepers alike, awakens glistening in the morning as though freshly whitewashed.

Arrange things locally with Saad, of Badawya Hotel in Farafra town. For cost of overnight trips into the White Desert in a six-person jeep, call mobile: 010 5364440.

Turquoise Mines

In Sinai, one of the best off-road adventures is to the **Wadi Magara turquoise mines**, which are reached by following an ancient track eastwards up Wadi Sidri from Abu Rudeis, midway down the west coast of the peninsula. At 25km Wadi Magara opens off to the north and it is then a short distance to the mines. They are round the final leftwards bend, 40m above the valley floor on the left.

The mines were worked as early as the First Dynasty, and as you walk deep into the valley wall you sometimes notice small turquoises, though these are of little value. If you climb higher you come to carvings on the rock face depicting 4th- and 5th-Dynasty pharaohs. Directly across the valley, on the hill opposite, are the remains of workshops, workers' houses, and a fort, all pharaonic. Back down on the sandy wadi floor you can picnic beneath the shade of an acacia tree.

At the eastern end of Wadi Sidri, head north 50km to the larger turquoise mines of **Serabit el Khadim**, where there is also a 12th-Dynasty sanctuary to Hathor. If you turn south at the end of Wadi Sidri, you enter, almost immediately, the broad **Wadi Moqattab**, the Valley of Inscriptions. Here you will find mostly Nabataean and Greek, but also Coptic and Arabic texts, dating from the 1st to 6th centuries AD.

In Cairo you can arrange jeep safaris into the Western Desert or to Sinai through Sahara Pioneer, 17 Latif Mansour, Heliopolis. Tel: (202) 2900989; Fax: (202) 2900186; saharapioneer@virtualoasis.com

Camels

You can also venture into the wadis of Sinai, and trek over the mountains, on camelback. Camels with guides can be hired at Dahab, Nuweiba, Sharm el Sheikh, and St Catherine's.

Treks usually take from one to ten days. Be prepared to produce a medical certificate, and have your own sleeping bag and first aid kit. You may be required to register your trip with the police for security purposes.

Egypt has three deserts. Sinai and the Eastern Desert are both, for the most part, broken, mountainous areas with some vegetation in the shelter of their deeply indented valleys. Bedouin (nomadic Arab herdsmen) inhabit both these regions. The Western Desert, an extension of the Sahara, is entirely different. Among the hottest and driest places in the world, it is a level plateau utterly without water or vegetation except where occasional springs surface at deep depressions to create oases. White sands, formed by the disintegrating rock strata, move in graceful, undulating dunes of awesome power, encroaching on fields and villages, submerging telephone poles and engulfing entire trucks. The mighty army of the 6th-century BC Persian king Cambyses was swallowed by the sands during an expedition to Siwa, and in 1805, a 2,000-strong camel caravan disappeared into the same sands.

The Living Desert

Animal life is dependent on vegetation, and so only the most specialised of species can inhabit the deserts. Even these are found mostly near oases or in the northern scrubland along the Mediterranean coast. Mammals include the gazelle, desert fox, hyena, jackal, and the gerbil. Migratory birds such as swallows, hoopoes, wagtails, and warblers pause in the oases during their flights, attracted by the abundant insect life. Snakes and lizards are more permanent residents; indeed the Egyptian cobra, *Naja haje*, is almost an ancient monument, having served as the uraeus on pharaonic crowns.

The animal perhaps most associated with the desert is the camel. Introduced from Asia, it became plentiful only during the Ptolemaic period. The ones you now see in Egypt are bred mostly in Sudan from where they are driven along the Darb el Arbain, the Forty Days' Road, from Darfur to the Tuesday morning camel market (*souk el Gamal*) at Daraw, 6km south of Kom Ombo.

Others continue by train to the Friday morning camel market at Birqosh, 35km northwest of Cairo.

Mount Sinai: sunrise from the summit (top); steps and arch on the old path up (above); tourists making their way down (facing page)

Feluccas

If you have not already sailed in a *felucca*, you will almost certainly do so in Aswân when you visit the islands in the Nile and the sites on the west bank (*see pp134–5*). You will rapidly discover that you have become addicted to its pleasure, and the only cure is to indulge in some more.

Excursion to Sehel

You could start with the half-day journey from Aswân to the island of Sehel and back. Though the current is against you as you head upstream, your boatman extends the gaff upwards, giving great height and grace to the sail, which then fills with the prevailing wind.

From the island there is a view of the rocks and swirling waters of the First Cataract, although the Nile hardly pounds and foams as once it did, before the building of the British dam. On the other hand, the ferocity of the sun as you step ashore should warn you how dangerous its rays really are, cool though you may feel as you sail along the river.

With its head into the wind, but taking advantage of the current, your *felucca* tacks back down the Nile. If you drink from the river, it is said, you will return to

Egypt. You might have thought you would drop dead instead. In fact, the Nile has a fresh and somewhat organic taste, and the boatmen drink from it all the time, saying there is no bilharzia above Esna, and certainly no danger of it from fast flowing water. On the other hand, they say tourists actually get upset stomachs from drinking ice-cold bottled water and soft drinks.

Drop Out for Five Days

The longer *felucca* journey between Aswân and Luxor requires some forethought and preparation. For one thing there is the choice of blowing upstream with the wind from Luxor to Aswân, or floating downstream from Aswân to Luxor on the current. The latter is more predictable, taking five days and four nights, and it can also be a bit cheaper,

TOURS

Agencies along the corniche at Aswân and Luxor may put together a party of six to eight people for a boat, though you are free to do that yourself. You can also decide on a shorter journey, overnight from Aswân to Kom Ombo, for example, if you are pressed for time. Find out the official rate first from the tourist office; the actual price that you finally agree with the *felucca* captain will depend on season (cheaper in summer) and demand, generally. Payment should be made only at the end of the trip. As an easier option, several adventure tour operators offer a *felucca* trip as part of their Egypt packages.

costing about LE100 per person aboard a six- or twelve-passenger vessel. Stops are made at Kom Ombo, Edfu, and Esna.

Generally, *feluccas* only go as far as Edfu, which will cost LE70 per person for three nights. No food is included, and there is no night sailing. For an extra sum, the captain, usually an English-speaking Nubian, will also provide food, though it would probably be a good idea if you supplemented this with your own supplies. Unless you are willing to drink from the Nile like the boatmen, also take along three litres of bottled water for each day of the journey. You will be sleeping either on planking aboard the *felucca*, or on the ground ashore. Nights can be chilly throughout most of the year, and downright cold during winter, so you will need warm blankets or a sleeping bag. Also keep a sweater for the evenings, insect repellent, and, remembering how misleading the feel of the breeze can be, some form of protection – sunscreen lotion, hat, etc – against the sun, which is all the more intense for being reflected off the water.

Feluccas moored up outside the Old Cataract Hotel at Aswân

Tour: Feluccas and Camels

From tropical gardens on Botanical Garden to desert sands on the West Bank, this journey of unusual variety near Aswân combines a taste of adventure with abundant moments of sheer delight.

Allow 4 hours.

The Aga Khan Mausoleum

Begin by hiring a felucca *below the terrace of the Old Cataract Hotel or along the Corniche el Nil (see map on p122).*

1 Botanical Garden

Keep an eye out for egrets and hoopoes wading among the rocks as you sail round the southern point of Elephantine Island. General Kitchener became Consul-General in Egypt in 1911, and this island was presented to him then. Here he indulged his passion for flowers, ordering plants from around the world. Now known as the Botanical Garden, it is pleasant to walk along its shady paths, enjoying its fragrances and the many brightly coloured birds (*see p116*).

Sail northwards to the bare hill on the west bank of the Nile.

2 Nobles' Tombs

A trek up a sandy path from the landing stage brings you to a line of tombs cut into the cliff face (*see p119*). They all date from the late Old Kingdom to the early Middle Kingdom and belonged to the governors, princes, and priests whose lives revolved around the control of the Nubian trade. The most interesting is the tomb of Sirenput II (Tomb 31), who was a governor of Aswân during the Middle Kingdom. An undecorated pillared hall leads, by way of a corridor lined with Osiris statues, to a smaller hall, its pillars and walls covered with paintings of Sirenput and his family. On the rear wall, Sirenput sits at a table, his son before him clutching flowers, while all around are wonderfully coloured hieroglyphics.

You now sail southwards to a cove where a path leads up to the gates of Aga Khan's Mausoleum. Unfortunately, the Mausoleum is not open to the public.

3 Aga Khan's Mausoleum

Aga Khan III lived at the white villa here, and was buried in the domed mausoleum just above it in 1957. His fine white Carrara marble tomb was carved in Cairo with geometric patterns and Quranic inscriptions.

He was spiritual leader of the Ismailis, a Shi'ite sect, and also a man of considerable wealth and weight. At his diamond jubilee in 1945 he was weighed against diamonds which were then distributed among his followers. His playboy son, Ali, predeceased him, and he was succeeded by his more earnest grandson Karim, Aga Khan IV. Aga Khan III's wife, the Begum, lies buried next to him.

Near the felucca *landing you can hire a camel for an accompanied ride to St Simeon's. Alternatively, you can walk across the soft sand in 20 minutes.*

4 St Simeon's Monastery (Deir Anba Samaan)

Fields and gardens once filled the desert valley leading from the Nile up to the monastery. That was until 1173, when the monks were driven out and their monastery ruined by Saladin who feared it might be used as a refuge for Christian Nubians during their forays into Egypt.

Built like a fortress in the 7th century, enough survives within St Simeon's 10m-high walls to create an evocative impression of the community which once flourished here. There is a roofless basilica with badly damaged paintings of Christ and various saints in its apses. Nearby rises a three-storey keep, off which were the living quarters, including a refectory, cells for 300 resident monks, and dormitories for hundreds more pilgrims, as well as bakeries and workshops (*see p116*). *Return to your* felucca *to sail back to Aswân.*

For practical information on the sights see pp116–19. Also, refer to the map on p122.

The Old Cataract Hotel was used as a backdrop for the film of Agatha Christie's *Death on the Nile*

Cruise: The Nile

To see Egypt from the deck of a cruise boat is one of the most pleasurable experiences of a lifetime. Although some boats cruise the Nile from Cairo to Aswân, most cruises are between Luxor and Aswân. These shorter cruises, which last from three to five days, often also include Dendera and Abydos to the north of Luxor.

Cruises might be in either direction, but the typical route described here is from Luxor north to Dendera and Abydos, and then south, passing Luxor, to Esna, Edfu, Kom Ombo, and Aswân. If your cruise begins at Aswân, follow this summary in reverse order.

1 Luxor

Board mid-afternoon. The following day take in the Temple of Luxor and Karnak on the east bank of the Nile, and the Theban necropolis on the west bank (*see pp92–107*). Sail north at evening, tying up at Dendera overnight.

2 Dendera

Buses are on hand for your visit to the Ptolemaic Temple of Hathor at Dendera (*see pp86–7*). The 1km walk along a country road leading straight to the temple is cool and beautiful, especially if it is early in the morning.

3 Abydos

Your boat may pass through the Nag Hammâdi barrage and under the railway bridge (so close a squeeze that the upper deck is cleared), to tie up off Abydos, but usually it remains at Dendera while buses transfer you to Abydos, and the

temple built by Seti I (*see pp84–5*). You then return to Dendera by bus, and sail southwards past Luxor, tying up overnight at Esna.

The romantic Nile cruise was invented by Thomas Cook

4 Esna

At Esna there is a barrage, built by the British in 1906–7, which serves also as a bridge. There is a newer lock, through which your boat must pass, but delays can still occur if too many boats wish to pass at the same time. This usually happens while you are asleep, or in the morning hours while you are visiting the Ptolemaic Temple of Khnum (*see pp110–11*).

5 Edfu

About midday you arrive at Edfu where you are met by carriages which take you to the huge Ptolemaic Temple of Horus (*see pp108–9*). Later in the day you sail south to Kom Ombo. Beyond Edfu the landscape changes, with the desert sometimes spilling down to the east bank of the Nile.

6 Kom Ombo

This double Temple of Sobek and Haroeris (Horus), also dating to the Ptolemaic period, enjoys a lovely setting on a low promontory overlooking the river (*see pp112–13*). You tie up beneath it and possibly spend the night here, sailing for Aswân in the morning.

The ribbon of cultivation on either side of the river is very thin now, and often the desert presses in on both sides. South of Kom Ombo much of the local population speaks the Nubian language, and it gives you the feeling that you are entering another world.

7 Aswân

You arrive in Aswân at midday (*see pp116–25*). It feels like sailing into an oasis. The town stands brightly on the east bank, and a great wave of desert rises on the west. Islands, *feluccas*, and granite outcrops seem to fill the Nile. There is something restful yet exciting about this place, as if you have finally reached the tropics.

The cost of the cruise includes visits to the sites en route. See pp162–3 for details.

Monasteries

Throughout their long history, Egypt's monasteries have been designed for getting away from it all. It was not to escape Roman persecution that early Christians fled to the deserts, rather to escape the fleshpots of the Nile. To stay overnight at a Coptic monastery is not exactly fun, but it is certainly an escape from modern living.

Fresco of St Paul

A pilgrim's account dating from the late 4th century describes Wadi Natrûn, known also as Scete: 'The place called Scete is set in a vast desert, and the way to it is to be found or shown by no track and no landmarks of earth, but one journeys by the signs and courses of the stars. Water is hard to find. Here are men made perfect in holiness, for so terrible a spot could be endured by none save those of austere resolve and supreme constancy'.

Demons and Fables

If this is not enough to challenge you, consider the demons you can rid your-self of. At the Monastery of Baramus the monks exhibit a shirt emblazoned with blood, its splatterings in the shape of numerous crosses. They tell you that not long ago a troubled man came to the monastery. On approaching the altar of God he shrank back in horror, and in a strange voice, he cursed the monks, who anointed him with oil on his wrists and head. This caused the devil to erupt from his body, splattering the shirt with blood as he went.

It is wonderful to be a child and to be told incredible bedtime stories. It is even more wonderful to be an adult and to sit beneath a vine trellis sipping tea within ancient walls somewhere in the darkening Western Desert, and to hear the incredible related from the lips of a bearded monk in a long black robe with a starry cowl pulled over his head. You are then shown to your quarters and advised to get to sleep early.

The Hermits

Baramus may well be the world's oldest, indeed the world's first monastery. It is surrounded by hermits' caves for those who find even monastic life too cosy; and as you lie in bed you think of them, alone in the Western Desert, practising humility through speaking to scorpions.

One such hermit was disturbed by bursting shells and a rain of shrapnel: the Battle of El Alamein was exploding around him. A startled soldier, seeing him emerge from his cave, nearly shot him dead. Even then the hermit would not move, declaring that the war was a devilish scheme to interrupt his prayers. When the smoke cleared, the British HQ in Cairo sent its apologies for the inconvenience caused.

A Section for Sinners

At 4am you are wakened by the sound of bells ringing through the desert air. You join the silent flow of robed figures who sweep across the moonlit courtyard of the monastery towards the ancient church. Here, amid dim candles and medieval icons, the day begins with two hours of chanting followed by three hours of liturgy in discordant Coptic and Arabic, enlivened occasionally by the tinkle of triangles.

Visitors are normally left at the outermost end of the nave, in the section reserved for sinners, where you can sleep through much of the chanting, and even creep away altogether. For the monks, however, their devotions are followed by an eight-hour day in the surrounding fields.

In case you arrived at Baramus looking for fun, there is a notice announcing that 'Looking at the wilderness kills the lusts of the soul. Visiting the monastery should be considered a trip of rebuke and not one for pleasure.'

See p178 for information on visiting Coptic monasteries.

The Coptic Monastery of St Paul (Deir Anba Bula), south of St Anthony's (Deir Anba Antunius)

Oases

To the ancient Egyptians the oases were gifts not of the Nile but of the sky. In fact, the four inner oases of the Western Desert mark the line of a prehistoric branch of the Nile, and to this day feed from ancient stores of underground water.

The ancients were not entirely wrong about the sky's role in creating the oases. *Wahat* (cauldron), was the pharaonic name for the depressions in which the oases sit. Eroded by winds in the course of millenia, the depressions dipped down towards the water table while atmospheric pressure caused the natural springs to bubble to the surface.

And so, as you pick your way along the hot, thin line of asphalt through a landscape of lethal immensity, you can imagine that these islands of fertility owe as much to the sky forces above as to the hidden waters below.

The Western Loop

A road over 1,000km in length loops far out into the Western Desert from Gîza, at first southwest to **Baharîya** and **Farafra** oases, continuing southeast to **Dakhla Oasis,** and then due east to **El Khârga Oasis**, before finally turning northeast to join the Valley of the Nile near Asyût. A road links El Khârga with Luxor, opening up the entire New Valley (as the governorate containing the four inner oases, but not distant Siwa, is called) to the large-scale tourism already attracted to Upper Egypt.

The oases are fascinating microcosms of Egyptian rural life and history, and they can serve as bases for short trips into the surrounding desert wilderness. You can explore one or two of them in a long weekend, or see them all in the course of a week's journey.

Baharîya and Farafra are the most inaccessible of the oases, and so best preserve their traditional feel. The native architecture is particularly handsome at Farafra, from where also you can visit the White Desert (*see p129*). Dakhla is probably the best single oasis to visit.

Date Palms and Gardens

The lush gardens and date groves of **Dakhla Oasis** strike a pleasing contrast with the surrounding pink and ochre rocks of the desert. It has large reserves of water, much of it brackish, and over 700 springs. At **Mut Talata**, 3km west of Dakhla's capital town of Mut, is a hot sulphur pool. Muddy brown and smelly, its effect on aching muscles is wonderful and you soon forget the aroma of rotten eggs. The best time to go is at night, when a layer of steam drifts across its surface and the sky is full of stars.

There is a lovely freshwater spring at **Bir el Gebel**, 35km west of Mut, and a 5km detour off the main road to El Qasr. Here you can feel that you are getting away even from the oasis. A few palm trees sprout beside the pool which is at the foot of Dakhla's 400m-high northern escarpment. From the top there is a marvellous view. In one direction are the villages of the oasis, in the other, below the escarpment, is a field of boulders smoothed into parallel, identical teardrops by the wind.

The old part of **El Qasr**, 40km north of Mut, is an all but abandoned fortress town of towers and domes rising from a hill, though when you are in it you seem to be underground. Its alleys were covered for shade and built low and narrow to force any invaders to dismount, making them vulnerable to ambush within the maze of passages and dead ends. The thick-walled houses jut with wooden beams. The door lintels of many are single blocks of beautiful dark wood, engraved with Quranic verses. You can fully explore two of the houses which have been renovated by the Egyptian Antiquities Organisation.

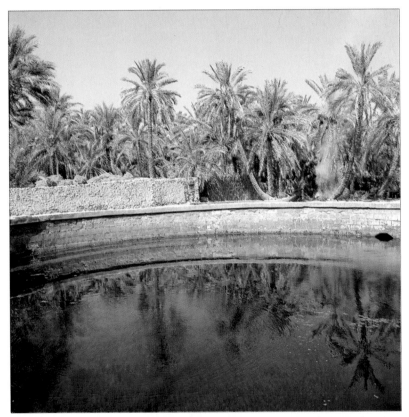

Brides used to take a ritual bath in Cleopatra's Spring, one of the many springs at Siwa Oasis

Red Sea Resorts

Coming to the Red Sea resorts does not necessarily mean getting away from anything. In fact, it can often mean stepping into the middle of tattiness and vulgarity. One reason for this is that most people who come are interested almost exclusively with what lies underwater, leaving developers free to ruin the landside environment.

Hurghada, on the mainland Egyptian coast, 372km south of Suez, is a prime example of this. Only the big resort hotels offer relief, though if you are not a diver or beach lover, there is so little to do that you should not plan on staying long.

The Best of Diving

The best stretch of coastline, both for divers and for the rest, is from **Ras Muhammad** at the southern tip of Sinai to **Taba**, 1km from the Israeli border. This is the **Gulf of Aqaba**, a northern extension of the Red Sea, rivalled only by Australia's Great Barrier Reef for the finest dive sites in the world. Its resorts are readily accessible, its sharks well fed enough to have no interest in eating you, and its landscape beautiful.

Ras Muhammad is an undeveloped nature preserve reached only by private vehicle or boat from Sharm el Sheikh. There are no camping facilities, yet it is over-crowded at weekends. **Sharm el Sheikh, Na'ama Bay, Dahab,** and **Nuweiba** are established holiday centres, offering camel treks, good swimming, and a variety of watersports.

Taba

Ever since the Israelis handed Taba over to the Egyptians in 1989, new hotels and resorts have sprung up along the coast to Sharm el Sheikh. The diving here and off Pharaoh's Island opposite is interesting. When Saladin captured the island from the Crusaders in 1170 he built the fortress, now restored, that you see upon it today. (*For more on the Red Sea resorts,* see pp76–7. *For the Reefs,* see pp160–61.)

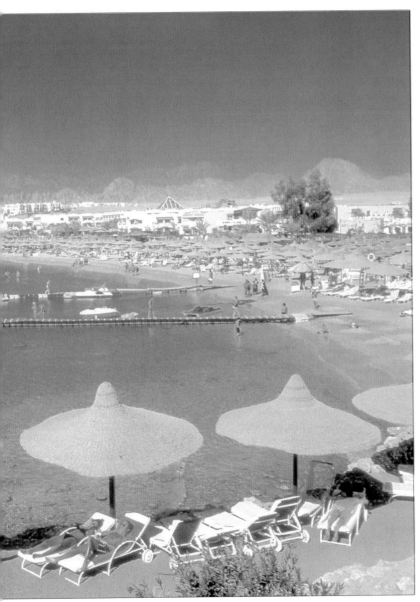

Touristy towns form the hinterland for the beaches along the Red Sea, ideal for sunbathing

Shopping

Simply to list Egypt's traditional crafts and wares brings to life the sights and scents of the bazaar: spices and perfumes, brass and copperware, gold and silver jewellery, glass, ceramics and precious stones, carpets, inlay work and *mashrabiyya*, cottons and leatherwork. Places like Cairo's Khan el Khalili and Aswân's Sharia el Souk are a browser's and shopper's dream. There is also the chance to buy antiquities at reputable shops both in Upper Egypt and in Cairo, and antiques from different periods at Alexandria's Rue Attarine.

A copy of exotic royal Egyptian jewellery

The country is, however, also moving with the times, and a new generation of craftsmen and designers is translating Egyptian themes into stylish and competitively priced clothing, jewellery, furnishings, household items, and so on, with an eye to international appeal. You will soon discover that shopping in Egypt is one of the best ways of getting to know the country.

Fixed-price department stores and most shops will display prices. The shops in the arcades of major hotels and shopping malls will mark prices in Western numerals; in local shops and department stores, prices are given in Arabic numerals, which is a good reason to become familiar with them (*see p28*).

Bargaining at Bazaars

You will discover that time is cheap in the bazaars of Egypt – cheap for Egyptians, if not for you. If you want to bargain well, you must be prepared to dedicate some time to it. A stallkeeper will always ask more than he expects to

get. The traditional response is to offer half as much. After several minutes, perhaps half an hour, a price midway between the extremes is agreed. That is the traditional way.

The virtue of a bazaar is that there is plenty of competition, and so, by shopping around, you ought to get a feel for price and be able to strike a good bargain. In Cairo's Khan el Khalili, for instance, you will find all the copperware in one area, all the spices in another, all the wood and mother-of-pearl inlay in yet another. This allows you to compare styles, quality, and price. It can be a good idea, also, to go to a fixed-price shop first – at least you will know the price you are out to beat.

It helps when bargaining if you appear dispassionate. The more that you show your interest, the more the seller is likely to make you pay for it. A good technique is to bargain first over something you do not want, and then casually to start bargaining over what you do want, almost as though you did not want anything and just bargained for the sport of it.

It is, in fact, a sport, and there are rules as well as tricks of the game. Your first extreme counter-offer will be laughed at and you may feel silly. Do not worry; that is only part of the game. If you feel that after several rounds of offers and counter-offers you are getting nowhere, walk out. The vendor will stop you if he thinks there is still a deal to be made. You can always go elsewhere.

The essence of a bargain, of course, is not to arrive at some preconceived fraction of the original asking price, but to feel that you have paid a price you could not have bettered elsewhere. It is a mark of your bargaining skills.

What to Buy
Alabaster
Vases, statuettes, and reproduction antiques such as scarabs are often carved from alabaster. The best place to shop is in Luxor, or workshops in the village of Gurna amid the Theban necropolis. All too frequently you will be pestered by touts offering you alabaster 'antiquities'; if you want one, offer only a tenth of the asking price.

Antiquities
Any antiquities offered to you on the street are bound to be fake, which is not to say there are no genuine pharaonic, Coptic, and Islamic artefacts around, although they are somewhat overpriced. However, it is illegal to export genuine antiquities.

Books and Prints
Books on Egypt and Egyptology, as well as facsimile prints of the work of such 19th-century artists as David Roberts, are available
in large bookshops in major tourist centres throughout the country. Cairo, however, is the place to look for originals of rare books and prints.

Brass and Copper
Brass and copper work has long been a Cairo tradition, and the standard is still high today. The finest items are the big brass trays which can serve as table tops, and for which wooden stands are available. More portable items include candlesticks, lamps, mugs, and pitchers, though be sure that anything you intend to drink out of is coated on the inside with another metal, like silver, as brass or copper can be highly poisonous in contact with some substances.

Camels
Most probably you will just want to browse and not buy at the Souk el Gamel in Cairo (particularly lively early Friday morning), or Daraw, near Kom Ombo in Upper Egypt, where the camels are brought for sale after being herded up from Sudan. The bargaining and trading are fascinating to watch.

Clothing and Fabrics
The *galabiyya*, the full-length traditional garment of Egyptian men, is popular with both male and female visitors as comfortable casual wear. Fancier versions can also serve as evening wear for women. There are three basic styles: the *baladi* or peasant style, with wide sleeves and a low rounded neckline; the *saudi* style, more form-fitting, with a

high-buttoned neck and cuffed sleeves; and the *efrangi* or foreign style, looking like a shirt with collar and cuffs, but reaching down to the floor.

A more recent phenomenon is designer fashion with international appeal. Prices of all clothing in Egypt will be lower than at home.

Egyptian cotton is the finest in the world, which is another good reason for buying Egyptian clothing, or having it made up for you. If you do, be warned that the workmanship is not always up to scratch, and you might have to make several return journeys. You may also like to buy locally manufactured and designed fabric, and ready-made clothes from international chains. Sizes are continental.

Glass

Muski glass, usually turquoise or dark brown and recognisable by its numerous air bubbles, has been handblown in Cairo for centuries. It is now turned out as ashtrays, candlesticks, and glasses.

Jewellery

Egyptian jewellery mostly mimics the more obvious pharaonic motifs such as the scarab (for good luck), cartouche, the *ankh* (the symbol of life), and the Eye of Horus.

Items of Islamic motif show little popular imagination, the designs usually confined to hands and eyes for warding off evil or being inscribed with 'Allah'. Anything outside these two motifs is usually conceived in bad taste. The exceptions are simple turquoise strands and Bedouin silverwork. Although the range of designs is limited, gold jewellery is a very popular souvenir for many visitors.

Leatherwork, Shoes, and Accessories

The most common items on offer are handbags, belts, suitcases, and hassocks, although Egyptian leather is not of the best quality.

Also, more interesting than comfortable are camel saddles. Shoes are possibly the major fashion retail item, and range from the highly stylish to cheap and practical. They do not wear as well as Western-made shoes, but the oriental leather slippers are a good buy.

Musical Instruments

Cairo is a good place to buy traditional musical instruments. These include the *oud* (lute), the *rabab* (viol), the *nai* (flute), the *kanoon* (dulcimer), the *tabla* (drum), the *mismare baladi* (oboe), and the *duf* and *riq* (forms of tambourine).

Nargilehs

You often see men smoking the *nargileh* or 'hubbly-bubbly' at cafés. A moist lump of tobacco is put into a small terracotta cup and is kept alight by a piece of glowing charcoal. By sucking on a flexible tube, the smoke is drawn down the stem of the pipe through a container of water which reduces tar and makes for a very mild smoke. The best *nargilehs* will have glass rather than brass bodies for holding the water.

Papyrus

The sheets of 'papyrus' sold with pharaonic scenes painted on them are often made from banana leaves. Real

Well stocked curio shop

papyrus can withstand being crumpled up; if the one you are offered cracks when you crumple it, do not buy it. You can see genuine papyrus being made at Dr Ragab's Papyrus Institute in Cairo (*see p149*) and at Luxor near the museum, where you can also buy it.

Scents and Spices

For a thousand years, Cairo has been one of the world's greatest centres for the trade in spices, which also explains its position as a purveyor of perfume essences, the aroma of history still pervading the markets of Khan el Khalili.

Egypt provides essences to French perfumiers who, apart from combining them in their own inimitable way, also dilute them in nostril-blasting alcohol. Egyptian perfume, on the other hand, is often made by diluting the essence in oil. You should not count on getting quite the scent you want, as that can take some time and mixing, but the experience is fun. Essences from musk

to rose and lotus flower are combined in intoxicating proportions with alcohol or oil. Scents, spices, and herbs for cooking and cures are also sold in Khan el Khalili, as well as in Aswân's souq.

Weavings, Carpets, Tents, and Tapestries

Egypt is not particularly renowned for its carpets, but Aswân is the best place to look around for small carpets and weavings of all sorts, which originate in neigbouring regions. Many of these have the bright sense of African colouring. Tent-making, on the other hand, is a Cairene speciality, and you will often see beautiful appliqué tents used in street festivals. Decorations may be figurative, on pharaonic or Islamic themes, but the best have abstract arabesque designs or intricate calligraphy. You don't have to buy a whole tent: they are made in sections, and you can buy a piece as a cushion cover.

Rural motifs and bold colours give the world-famous tapestries of Harraniyya, a village near Gîza, their naive charm. They are the creations of children who are taught traditional crafts at the Wissa Wassef Art School, which makes for an interesting visit.

Woodwork and Inlay

Cairene craftsmen are known for their wooden trays, game boards, and boxes intricately inlaid with mother-of-pearl and coloured bits of wood which are surprisingly cheap. *Mashrabiyyas*, those wonderfully carved wooden screens found in old Cairene houses, occasionally appear in the bazaars where they can often fetch a fairly high price.

Where to Buy

Almost everything you might want to buy is available in Cairo, in some cases only in Cairo. Certain places may have their special attractions, the souq in Aswân for example, or the Rue Attarine flea market in Alexandria, but you cannot beat Cairo for its range of stores and boutiques, and for its labyrinthine Khan el Khalili, with its exotic medieval atmosphere.

In Upper Egypt and at the Red Sea resorts, a range of reputable jewellers, clothiers, and the like will be found in the shopping arcades of major hotels, but here, and in Alexandria, there are no shops worth singling out. Just stick to the hotels, or head towards the market.

CAIRO
Antiquities
Ahmed Dahba
5 Sikket el Badestan, in the heart of Khan el Khalili.

Books and Prints
American University in Cairo (AUC) Bookstore
In Hill House on the university campus, 113 Sharia Qasr el Aini, near Midan el Tahrir.
Tel: (202) 7942964.
Lehnert and Landrock
44 Sharia Sherif, downtown.
Tel: (202) 3935324.
L'Orientaliste
15 Sharia Qasr el Nil, downtown.
Tel: (202) 5753418.

Brass and Copper
The shops in the Coppersmiths' Bazaar are the places for brass and copperware. You will find both these items at the western end of Khan el Khalili, along Sharia Muizz, between Sharia Muski and the Madrasa of Sultan Qalaun.

Camels
The camel bazaar, Souq el Gamel, is at Birqash beyond the Imbaba district of northwest Cairo, and is best reached by taxi. The market is held every Friday from 6am; the activity is pretty much over by 9am. Docile females are the preferred mounts, for which you should expect to pay LE2,500.

Reproduction of an original painting on papyrus

Clothing and Fabrics

Abbas Higazi
Top quality ready-to-wear and tailor-made traditional garments.
Khan el Khalili

Ammar
Good quality traditional *galabiyya*.
26 Sharia Qasr el Nil.

Atlas
Ready-to-wear, made-to-measure clothes, and fabrics also available.
Sikket el Badestan, at the heart of Khan el Khalili.
Tel: (202) 5924730.

Nomad
Bedouin designs adapted to Western styles.
Marriott Hotel, Zamalek.
Tel: (202) 7358888.
14 Sariya el Gezira, Zamalek.
Tel: (202) 7362132.

Omar Effendi
Good department store.
Downtown branches on Sharia Talaat Harb just off Midan el Tahrir, and on Sharia Adli near Sharia Talaat Harb.

On Safari
Stylish clothing.
10 Sharia Lutfalla, Zamalek.
Tel: (202) 7351909.

World Trade Centre
A new four-storey shopping centre, with well-known brand names.
Just north of the 26 July Bridge at 1191 Corniche el Nil, Boulaq.

Gifts

Khan Misr Toulon
Opposite Ibn Tulun Mosque, and just up the street from Gayer-Anderson House.
17 Ahmed Ibn Tulun St, Near Citadel.
Tel: (202) 3652227.

Jewellery

Nomad
Bedouin jewellery.
Marriott Hotel, Zamalek.
Tel: (202) 7358888.
14 Saraya el Gezira.
Tel: (202) 7362132.

Saad of Egypt
Silver.
Ramses Hilton.
Tel: (202) 5754999.
Khan el Khalili.
Tel: (202) 5893992.

Sirgany
Gold.
Sharia el Sagha, Khan el Khalili.
Tel: (202) 5901255.

Leather, Shoes, and Accessories
There is a plethora of bags, belts, suitcases, and shoe shops on Sharias 26 July, Talaat Harb, and Kasr el Nil, while leather goods and accessories are widely sold in Khan el Khalili market.

Musical Instruments
Shops sell traditional instruments on Sharia el Qa'la between Midan Ataba and the Islamic Art Museum.

Papyrus

Dr Ragab's Papyrus Institute
On a houseboat moored south of the Giza Sheraton.
Tel: (202) 3488676.

Scents and Spices
Khan el Khalili's spice and perfume bazaars are in the southeast quadrant formed by the intersection of Sharia el Muizz and Sharia el Muski, though spilling beyond.

Weavings, Carpets, Tents, and Tapestries
The tent-makers' bazaar is on Sharia Muizz, immediately south of Bab Zuwayla.

Senouhi
All kinds of carpets – an exclusive outlet for Harraniyya tapestries.
5th floor, 54 Sharia Abdel Khalek Sarwat, downtown.
Tel: (202) 3910955.

Woodwork and Inlay

Mother-of-Pearl Products
6 Khan el Khalili.

Entertainment

With the almost complete disappearance of its formerly cosmopolitan population since the 1950s, the range, quantity, and distribution of entertainment in Egypt has become much reduced. Alexandria, once full of Greeks, Italians, Jews, English, French, and others, now has virtually no nightlife or cultural activity that the passing visitor would notice. With the exception of Cairo, the same is true throughout the country, unless a luxury hotel lays on a tourist show. In Cairo there is entertainment until the early hours, and it is a special pleasure at the end of a long night out to see the sun come up while the calls for dawn prayers echo across the city.

Dancing in the traditional Egyptian way

Many well-to-do Egyptians with Western interests attend ballet, opera, and other concerts at Cairo's Opera House. Foreign cultural centres such as the British Council offer films, music, and theatre. It is even possible to go tenpin bowling and ice-skating.

However, visitors on a short stay may not have the time or inclination to seek these events out. Folk entertainments are still staged, in specialist theatres and large hotels, but more rewarding can be those genuine manifestations of popular culture, the *moulids* and other festivals (*see pp22–3*).

Visitors, therefore, should understand that even in Cairo the hotels are the best bet for entertainment, and that outside Cairo there is virtually nowhere else to go. The monthly magazine *Egypt Today* and the weekly English-language edition of *Al-Ahram* will give you a fairly good idea of what is going on.

What's on Offer

Almost all bars are within hotels or form part of a restaurant or nightclub. Many will have some form of entertainment. While the consumption of alcohol is legal, it is illegal to serve Egyptians (be they Copts or Muslims) during Ramadan or other festivals, which means bars not in international hotels are likely to be closed then.

Casinos

Admission to casinos, found in many major hotels, is restricted to non-Egyptians. The currency to play is US dollars, with free drinks to punters. Doors close at dawn.

Cinemas

English-language films are frequently shown, subtitled in Arabic. Sometimes the Egyptian audience, being able to read the subtitles, does not have to listen to the dialogue, but chatters away instead, making it difficult for others to hear, but audiences are becoming better-behaved. Prices are very reasonable.

Discos

Almost all discos are at the major hotels, and many of these are restricted to guests or members. Women will usually have no trouble entering alone, but men will often find that they cannot enter without a woman. You should phone first to check.

Egyptian Dance and Music

El Jeel is the rhythmic pop music of Egypt, a blend of Nubian, Bedouin, and Libyan beats. Live performances are sometimes included in nightclub programmes at Cairo's major hotels, or downtown, or along the Pyramids Road. Classical Arab music is presented at Cairo's Sayed Darwish Concert Hall in

Gîza, while folkloric music and dance is presented at the Balloon Theatre in the Cairo district of Agouza.

Nightclubs

The best nightclubs are found in Cairo's main international hotels. They usually offer a programme of both oriental and Western acts, for example, a first-class Egyptian belly dancer between thick slices of second-rate pseudo-Las Vegas showgirl acts. A four-course dinner is served from about 8pm onwards, the belly dancer usually coming on late, at about 11pm. Reservations are required.

Opera, Ballet, and Theatre

The Cairo Opera House is home to the Cairo Ballet Company and the Cairo Symphony Orchestra, and is the venue for visiting operas, plays, and musicals. Special events are often staged at the Pyramids, for example, operas.

Inhibitions are set aside while merry-making in a nightclub

Where to Go

Entertainment in Cairo is not hard to find with bars, discos, restaurants, and nightclubs aplenty to suit all tastes. Opera, ballet, concerts, and theatre are all on offer. For detailed information, a publication worth buying is *Cairo's Top 600*, a guide to drinking, dining, and dancing.

Bars

Barrel Lounge
A pleasant atmosphere and an interesting variety of clientele.
First floor, Windsor Hotel, Sharia Alfi Bey.

Johnny's Pub
A bustling place for the young and not so young.
Le Pacha boat, Saraya El Gezira, Zamalek.
Tel: (202) 7356730.

Absolute
Popular bar with music.
9 Amman Square, Mohandessin.
Tel: (202) 7497326.

Pub 28
Modelled on the traditional British pub.
28 Shagar el Durr, Zamalek.

Taverne du Champ de Mars
Rebuilt from an original Brussels bar.
Nile Hilton Hotel, Midan el Tahrir.
Tel: (202) 5780444.

Windows on the World
Fantastic views over Cairo.
Ramses Hilton Hotel, Corniche el Nil, Boulaq.
Tel: (202) 5777444.

Casinos

Le Casino
El Gezirah Sheraton Hotel, Zamalek.
Tel: (202) 7373737.

The Casino
Busy until the early hours.
Nile Hilton Hotel, Corniche el Nil, downtown.
Tel: (202) 5780444.

Casino Semiramis
Semiramis Intercontinental Hotel, Corniche el Nil, Garden City.
Tel: (202) 7957171.

Omar Khayyam Casino
Cairo Marriott Hotel, Zamalek.
Tel: (202) 7358888.

Cinemas

Cairo has a plethora of cinemas in a number of locations – hotels, shopping malls, downtown, and the suburbs, all showing the latest American and British films, as well as Egyptian productions. The foreign cultural

Popular film hoarding

centres, for example the British Council (*192 Sharia el Nil, Agouza, Tel: (202) 3453281*), and the American Cultural Center (*4 Sharia Ahmed Regheb, Garden City, Tel: (202) 3549601*), sometimes show films.

Discos

Jackie's
A disco situated in the 5-star Nile Hilton.
Nile Hilton Hotel, Midan el Tahrir.
Tel: (202) 5780444.

Regina
Of Paris, London, and New York fame.
El Gezirah Sheraton Hotel, Zamalek.
Tel: (202) 7373737.

Coco Jungle
A disco on the same boat as Johnny's Pub with good music and a good crowd.
Saraya El Gezira, Zamalek.
Tel: (202) 7356730.

Egyptian Music and Dance

Balloon Theatre
Venue for the National Troupe and the Reda Troupe, both folk dance troupes.
Sharia 26 July at Sharia el Nil, Agouza.
Tel: (202) 3471718.

Sayed Darwish Concert Hall
Venue for the Arabic Music Troupe.
Gamal el Din el Afghani, near the City of Art.
Tel: (202) 5612473.

Nightclubs

Abu Nawas
Western singer.
Mena House Oberoi Hotel, Pyramids Road, Giza.
Tel: (202) 3833222.

Arizona
If you are looking for the bottom of the barrel, this is it: sagging bellies and other grotesqueries.
El Haram Street.

La Belle Epoque
French flavour.
Meridien Hotel, Roda Island. Tel: (202) 3621717.

Haroun el Rashid
A different show every night.
Semiramis Intercontinental Hotel, Corniche el Nil, Garden City. Tel: (202) 7957171.

El Leil
Rather down-market, non-luxe bar, and belly dancing show.
El Haram Street, Giza.

Opera, Ballet, and Theatre

Cairo Opera House
A Japanese-designed complex. The ballet season is from January onwards, opera from March onwards, and the symphony orchestra season from September through to June.
Gezira.
Tel: (202) 7370601.

Gumhuria Theatre
Plays in various languages including English, French, and Arabic.
12 Sharia Gumhuria, downtown.
Tel: (202) 3919956.

Wallace Theatre
English-language plays and musicals, as well as concerts, during the academic year from October through to May.
American University in Cairo, Sharia Kasr el Aini, off Midan el Tahrir.
Tel: (202) 7942964.

The Cairo Ballet Company and Symphony Orchestra perform in the Cairo Opera House

A dancing baboon, a woman breathing fire, a man staging a backstreet performance involving a snake and a guinea pig, these are among the forms of entertainment you might come across on the streets of Cairo or Alexandria. Weddings are also a public spectacle, the parade of ululating women, tambourine-playing men, usually a belly dancer, too, preceding the bashful bride and groom. The form is similar whether along the streets of the poorer quarters, or through the lobby of a luxury hotel.

You might sit at a café like Fishawi's in Khan el Khalili and listen to a gypsy woman singing a wailing song, or go to a low dive like the Arizona at the Midan Orabi end of Sharia Alfi to watch belly dancers who've seen better days. A zany finger-cymbal player is followed by a

nonchalant Lebanese riding a unicycle across a wire 2 metres above the stage. What is common to all these entertainments, the puppet shows, the story tellings, and the dervish hoppings that accompany every *moulid*, is the abandoned enjoyment with which they are each equally received.

It is perhaps this playfulness, together with a flair for the melodramatic and a touch of African oomph, that makes Egyptians the leading film makers, actors, dancers, and singers in the entire Arab world.

The long-robed Kuwaitis, Saudis, and Sudanese are not in the big city to attend the El Azhar; they have come for fun. Cairo has long been the Hollywood, the La Scala, the Motown, and the Las Vegas of the Middle East. Even in the warble of the muezzins there is a virtuosity unheard elsewhere. It can be traced back to the drones and chants of the Coptic Church, some of whose own hymns almost certainly preserve something from forms of ancient pharaonic worship.

Performances of traditional music and dance can be seen in the major hotels, some of which also have casinos

Children

Egyptians are extremely indulgent towards children, and you will find that they are welcomed everywhere, including hotels and restaurants, mosques, and archaeological sites. It is this lack of fussiness towards children, however, that can expose a child to accident. Be alert to untended excavations and traffic, for example, and be sure that your children observe careful hygiene, and are well protected with clothing, hats, and sunglasses against the sun. The better hotels can usually provide childminders, and medical services are excellent.

Bedouin girl from Siwa Oasis

Children may well take more readily to the strangeness of their environment than you do, and they will probably find the dress, the scent, and the bustle of the bazaar more interesting than a museum or tomb. Carriage and camel rides, and sailing in a *felucca* are particular favourites. Sound and light shows will be mysterious and fun. Floating and outdoor restaurants will seem novel, and certain theme eating places out by the pyramids have been designed with children very much in mind. Additionally, there are a number of attractions – pharaonic villages and the like with a local flavour – which are aimed especially at children.

Aquarium Grotto

Numerous marine tanks spread along a labyrinth of passageways in the Grotto, referred to as the fish garden, contain nearly 200 varieties of fascinating tropical fish and sea creatures.
Galabaya Park, Zamalek. Open: daily 8.30am–3.30pm. Admission charge.

Cairo Puppet Theatre

Puppet shows regularly held here, including old favourites like *Ali Baba* and *Sinbad*, are in Arabic. It hardly matters, though, as it is very easy to follow the action, and it somehow adds to the enchantment of the productions, which will appeal to adults and children alike.

The season is from October through to May, with nightly performances at 6.30pm, as well as Friday and Saturday shows at 11am.
Midan Ataba at the southeast end of Ezbekieh Gardens, downtown.
Tel: (202) 5910954.

Cairo Zoo

An extensive and well-stocked zoo – the finest in the world when it was founded a century ago – but sadly not very well kept now. There are hundreds of varieties of marine aquaria with exotic tropical fish. There are also camel rides.
Gîza. Open: daily 6am–5pm.
Admission charge.

Cookie Amusement Park

Rides and games.
*Near the Gîza Pyramids. Open: daily
3–11pm, from noon on Fri.*

Dr Ragab's Pharaonic Village

A two-hour tour takes you round a
replica temple and nobleman's villa, and
floats you along the Canal of Mythology
where you encounter the ancient gods.
Costumed Egyptians perform
appropriate priestly and domestic tasks.
There is also a mock-up of King
Tutankhamun's tomb, several museums,
a playground, and a restaurant.
*Jacob Island. Tel: (202) 5718675. Reached
by half-hourly boats from the Corniche el
Nil, 2km south of Gîza Bridge.
Open: daily 9am–9pm. Admission charge,
children under six, free access.*

Felfela Village

An offshoot and expansion of the
original Felfela restaurant in central
Cairo. This rambling outdoor
entertainment complex is popular with
children, and has a restaurant,
playground, camel rides, a puppet show
and zoo, plus a programme including
acrobats, music, belly dancers, and
dancing horses.
*Maryotteya Canal, Gîza.
Tel: (202) 3841111. Open: daily 10am–
7pm. Entertainment from noon–6pm;
daily in summer; Tue, Fri, Sat, and Sun
in winter. Admission charge.*

National Circus

A good one-ring affair with the usual
animals, acrobats, and clowns.
*Next to the Balloon Theatre at Agouza, by
the 26 July Bridge. Tel: (202) 3470612.*

*Daily performances from 9.30pm.
Admission charge.*

Sinbad Amusement Park

Bigger than the Cookie Amusement
Park near the pyramids, this has bumper
cars, a roller-coaster, and other rides.
*Near Cairo Airport. Open: summer,
daily 5pm–2am, winter, daily 2–11pm,
except Fri when it opens at 10am.
Admission charge.*

El Urman Gardens

These former gardens of the khedives of
Egypt provide plenty of space for kids to
enjoy a picnic after a visit to the zoo.
*Gîza, opposite Cairo Zoo. Open: daily
8am–8pm, closes Thu at noon, and all
day Fri.
Admission charge.*

Friendly and curious

Sport and Leisure

Apart from the Red Sea resorts, with their almost exclusive concentration on diving activities, the main centre for sport is Cairo, which provides well for visitors wanting to keep fit or have fun. However, in most tourist resorts, for example, Luxor, Sharm, and Hurghada, tennis and golf are both available.

Snorkelling and swimming in the Red Sea

The All-Round Choice

The best all-round place is the Gezira Sporting Club, the oldest and most distinguished club in Cairo. Founded in 1888, it was built primarily for the British and a select number of Egyptians, and offered, then as now, such sports as polo and croquet. With the 1952 revolution, however, most foreign members were thrown out, and Egyptians were more freely admitted, although today it still has more foreign members than any other club in Cairo.

The Club has many sports to offer, but visitors are restricted to taking part in just two: golf and horse racing. There is a nine-hole golf course with a small pro shop where you can hire equipment. Horse racing takes place every alternate Saturday and Sunday (every other Saturday it is at the Heliopolis Hippodrome). The standard of racing is not quite what one would expect, but is nevertheless an interesting experience. Visitors may enter the club and walk around the various tracks and paths, or simply have a refreshing drink in one of the eating outlets.

Gezira Sporting Club, Sharia Gezira, Zamalek. Tel: (202) 7352272.
Open: 7am–11pm. Admission charge.

Cycling

The **Cairo Cyclists** (*Tel: (202) Eddi Gough on 7350069*) meet every Friday at 8am at the front gate of the Cairo American College, 1 Midan Digla. The route and pace is decided by those joining the ride, but can be up to 30–40 miles. Participants can branch off at will.

Diving

The **Cairo Divers Group** (*tel: (202) 4176515 9am–3pm and 6–9pm*) meets on the first Monday of each month at Nautilus Divers, 4 Omar Shaaban St, Ard el Golf, Heliopolis. Its more than 300 members of 11 nationalities have joined together to promote the exploration of the Red Sea. Meetings are open to all.

Golf

There are about a dozen golf courses in Cairo, and at major resorts around Egypt, many of them championship class. One of the oldest, the Mena House course, is a well-watered oasis beneath the brown of the Pyramids. However, one of the best courses in Cairo is **Mirage**, an 18-hole course on the outskirts of the city and, like its near neighbour, purpose-built in the desert. Both Mirage and **Katamaya** have opulent club houses with attendant health club facilities, and swimming and tennis at the latter, and, eventually, at the former. Both clubs are around 25km from Cairo city centre.

Out of Cairo, there are some stunning courses, most notably at Soma Bay on the Red Sea, and further north, the course at El Gouna.

Mirage City Golf Club, Ring Road, new Cairo. Tel: (202) 4091464.

Health Clubs

All the luxury-class hotels have health clubs. Hotel residents have automatic temporary membership; many admit non-residents on a daily or weekly basis.

Nile Hilton Health Club

Facilities include a gymnasium, sauna, swimming pool, and tennis courts.

Nile Hilton Hotel, Midan el Tahrir. Tel: (202) 5780444. Open: daily 10am–10pm. Charges vary according to facility used.

Splash

Swimming pool, Jacuzzi, floodlit tennis courts, health food bar, etc.

Marriott Hotel, Zamalek. Tel: (202)

7358888. Open: daily 6am–11pm. Charges vary according to facility used.

Running

The **Hash House Harriers** meet every Friday afternoon at about two hours before sunset for non-competitive fun runs at the Pyramids in the desert, and through the more traffic-free parts of town. Members include people of all nationalities, ages, sexes, regardless of ability. *Tel: Mathew at (202) 3595577; Paul 3576041, for a recorded message. www.cairohash.com*

Spectator Sports

Football, Horse Racing, and Rowing

Information on spectator sports is found in the newspaper *The Egyptian Gazette (The Egyptian Mail)*.

Egypt's favourite sport is football. The two main teams are Zamalek and Ahly. From September through to May, games are played every weekend (Friday–Sunday) at the Cairo Stadium in Heliopolis. There is horse racing from October to May at the Gezira Sporting Club and the Heliopolis Hippodrome.

Green lung in the heart of the city – a lush golf course

The Red Sea offers perfect conditions for the growth of coral. As well as having a high water temperature, which in itself promotes growth, the depth of the Red Sea prevents surface waves from affecting reef development. No major rivers spill into the sea, so its waters are exceptionally clear, allowing sunlight to penetrate deeply. As a result, Red Sea reefs extend deeper than in most other coral areas.

Most visiting divers stay within the fringe reef. A shallow sandy lagoon extends from the shoreline to the reef crest, a zone often too shallow for fish to cross. It is commonly the home of organ pipe corals. Beyond this is the reef slope, which is usually very steep and occasionally overhanging, with deep caves and canyons. Here, there are massive banks of mountain and staghorn corals. Further out, the fore reef now descends more gradually, almost horizontally, covered by unusual coral formations which can rise close to the surface.

Corals

Coral reefs constitute the most complex community of animals and plants in the sea. Many species of fish, from jewel-like damselfish to brightly spotted snappers, make their home here, taking advantage of the abundance and variety of food organisms, as well as the shelter the reef affords from predators, although some, such as the ferocious moray eel, do lurk in its crevices.

Adjacent seagrasses are important as a nursery ground for many reef fishes, while fish living in the sand flats beyond, such as rays or lizardfish, are either protectively coloured to look like sand, or they actually bury themselves in it.

Rules

• To preserve the fragile reefs, the rule, enforced by law is never to take anything out of them dead or alive.

• For your own safety, you should wear protective covering on your feet, you should not touch the coral, and you should not swim alone.

• Never buy products made from reef creatures.

The Red Sea reefs are home to a fascinating array of marine life

Cruising

Taking a cruise along the Nile is a time honoured tradition. It can be the journey of a lifetime and is one of the best ways of seeing the ancient sites in Upper Egypt. For the adventurous, sailing along the Nile in a *felucca* is the thing (*see pp132–3*). If you prefer not to trust to sail and sleeping bag, there is the comfort of the traditional cruise. A Nile cruise may form part of an overall package, or you may be an independent traveller who wants to include a cruise in your plans. It is possible to arrange both from abroad and, indeed, it would be wisest if you did so. Once in Egypt, you will be leaving it to the last moment and you will have to take whatever, if anything, is available.

THOMAS COOK NILE CRUISES

Thomas Cook invented the romantic Nile cruise. Among its cruises on its own boats, the latest is MS *Prince Abbas*. Book through any Thomas Cook travel agency world-wide, or direct from: Thomas Cook Holidays, PO Box 5, 12 Coningsby Rd, The Thomas Cook Business Park, Peterborough PE3 8XP, UK (*tel: 01733 41700*).

Travel agencies such as Thomas Cook or the Egyptian agency Misr Travel can make the arrangements either in Egypt or abroad (*see pp186–7*). Cruise operators include Thomas Cook (*see box*), Eastmar, Presidential Nile Cruises, Abercrombie & Kent, Explore Worldwide, Kuoni, and Swan Hellenic. Several groups also operate cruises which can be booked through their hotels or reservation centres.

Prices

Prices are highest from October to May, falling by about 10 per cent in summer, and include meals, sightseeing ashore, taxes, and service charges. For a five-day cruise on one of the international hotel chain boats, expect to pay about $1,500 per double cabin during high season, and about $1,100 during low season. Local operators offer cruises at substantially lower rates.

Floating Hotels

The international hotel boats, known as 'floating hotels', are the behemoths of

Entertainment, Egyptian style, is a main feature of nightlife on board the boat

the Nile. With 50 to 80 cabins, bars, boutiques, swimming pools, hairdressers, and discos, they can leave you uncertain that you ever left dry land. You may feel, however, that their luxury, and the number of people on board, gets in the way of the experience.

Often the smaller the boat, the better the ambience. There are several vessels of 20 to 30 cabins that are used both by local and overseas operators, and time and again it is these less prepossessing craft which win the most enthusiastic reactions from travellers.

The Itinerary

A cruise on the Nile, seeing life along its banks, makes a profound cumulative effect on you. There are innumerable cruise boats on the Nile, the majority plying between Luxor and Aswân, and calling at Esna, Edfu, and Kom Ombo. Some loop northwards from Luxor to visit Dendera and Abydos. Most cruises are four to eight days long, though half that time is spent moored at Luxor or Aswân while you trot round the local sites. Sadly, the full cruise between Cairo and Aswân is currently suspended, with no plans to reinstate it. All cruises include the services of an Egyptian guide who will be trained in archaeological history, but their quality can be variable. Some foreign-organised cruises will also include the services of a qualified Egyptologist who will give lectures and can answer questions. Enquire closely to ensure that your cruise provides you with the level of scholarly back-up that you want.

One of the many floating hotels that ply the Nile between Luxor and Aswân

Food and Drink

From simple village fare to classic Turkish cuisine, with Greek, Lebanese, and French influences, Egyptian food is as varied as the country's history, geography, and social structure. Most hotels in Egypt, however, cater to the tastes of foreign visitors by serving an international cuisine, so that if you want to immerse yourself in the full variety of Egyptian cooking you need to venture forth to the multitude of restaurants serving from the humblest to the most exquisite meals. A dining guide to Cairo's top five hundred restaurants can be purchased in hotel book shops and all good stationers.

A quiet smoke on the *nargileh*

Variety of Choice

Typically, dishes will be savoury, neither too oily nor too spicy, and because only fresh ingredients will be used, the menu will vary with the season. Nubian cooking, in the south of Egypt, tends to be spicier; Alexandrian cuisine is Mediterranean. In Cairo, the choice is almost limitless.

Eating places can be divided into four broad categories. There are Western-style restaurants which generally aim at a diluted or internationalised French cuisine. They will have a correspondingly wide-ranging menu. Then there are speciality restaurants – Greek, Chinese, Italian, Indian, or those pretending to be a pharaonic barge – which tend to offer one fare, with some variations and alternatives. Also, there are Middle Eastern restaurants which run the gamut from simple Egyptian fare through to Levantine, which can be a mixture of Egyptian, Turkish, French,

and other cuisines. In addition, there are cafés where you can get a light meal. Egypt has its fair share of fast food restaurants, and these proliferate from Alexandria to Aswân. Wherever and whatever you decide to eat, be scrupulous about hygiene, and never eat anything that has been lying around, or is improperly cooked or washed.

National Dishes

Egypt's national dishes are *fool*, a paste made from the fava bean to which oil, lemon, salt, and pepper are usually added. *Tamaiya* (*felafel*) is made from the same beans, but in this case they are pressed into a patty and fried in oil. *Tahina* is a sesame paste, while *babaganouh* is a paste made from eggplant. *Koushari* is a delicious mixture of rice, macaroni, lentils, and chickpeas, topped with a spicy sauce. Meat usually comes as kebabs and *kofta*, a spicy ground meat patty.

One or several of these dishes will be the entire offering of the simplest Egyptian eating places. Probably there will be no menu, but you can always go into the kitchen, have a look, a taste, and then point to what you want.

As these are national dishes, you will probably find them, even if only as hors d'oeuvres, on the menu of almost any restaurant in the country.

Drinks

Turkish style coffee, thick and black, is ordered according to the amount of sugar: sweet (*ziyada*), medium (*mazboota*), or bitter (*saada*). Western-style brewed coffee is usually called 'French coffee', while instant coffee is almost always known as 'Nescafe' whether it is or not. Tea is generally understood as mint tea or Indian tea, but usually without milk.

Western-style soft drinks, including Coca-Cola and 7-Up, are available everywhere. Egypt scores well on tropical fruit and cane juices. Tap water in the towns is heavily chlorinated, and so it is more for reasons of taste than safety that you might prefer to buy bottled mineral water.

Stella beer in the green bottle is very good. Stella Export in the brown bottle is sweeter, more consistent, more expensive, but not as good. Egyptian wines are drinkable. *Omar Khayyam* is a dry red, *Cru des Ptolemees* a dry white, and *Rubis d'Egypte* a rosé. The Obelisk range competes favourably with these. Imported beers, wines, and spirits are very expensive.

Egypt makes its own spirits, but the gin is undrinkable, the brandy compares with the Spanish variety, while *arak* (the Arab equivalent of Greek *ouzo*) is excellent, whether neat, on the rocks, or diluted with water.

Regional dishes served the Egyptian way

Where to Eat

In Upper Egypt and at the Red Sea resorts it is the hotels which offer the best eating places, although there are now more and more independent restaurants springing up in these areas. Unfortunately, some are dull and, in several cases, definitely unacceptable. However, in Cairo and, to a lesser extent, Alexandria, there is a wide choice of cuisine and atmosphere.

Cairo is more expensive than Alexandria, and generally hotel restaurants are more expensive than others. Drinks in hotels are generally fairly expensive, and a bottle of wine can be more than double the retail cost.

Generally speaking, a bottle of wine will retail at about LE30 in one of the special shops licensed to sell alcohol. A bottle of really good wine with a meal might cost in the region of LE60, becoming slightly cheaper according to the standard of the restaurant.

The following ratings will give a rough indication of the cost of a two-course meal for one person, without alcohol:

★   cheap LE15–30.
★★   mid-range LE30–75
★★★   expensive LE75–140

ALEXANDRIA
Western-Style Food
El Farouk ★★★
Very stylish, fine dining with a French flavour, the restaurant is in the El Salamlek Palace Hotel, situated in the beautiful grounds of the Montazah Palace.
Montazah Palace Gardens, Montazah.
Tel: (203) 5477999.
Delta Hotel Restaurant ★★
Excellent French cuisine.
14 Sharia Champollion, Mazarita.
Tel: (203) 4829053.
Lord's Inn ★★★
Posh, romantic, and good food.
Sharia Mohammed Ahmed el Afifi, San Stefano.
Tel: (203) 5865664.
Santa Lucia ★★
An older popular restaurant that includes a good seafood menu.
40 Sharia Safiya Zaghlul.
Tel: (203) 4820372.
Tikka Grill and Fish Market ★★
The best setting in Alexandria, with marvellous views over the

ALCOHOL IN EGYPT

The consumption of alcohol is legal in Egypt, though an Egyptian cannot buy a drink during Ramadan, and some governorates, for example Suez, are dry all year round. Neither EgyptAir nor the railways serve alcoholic drinks. That being said, alcoholic drinks are readily available at hotels and most restaurants – ask and you will receive. Beer, wine, and spirits are hard to buy and are only sold in specially licensed shops. Spirits are perhaps best avoided, as there have been instances of adulterating the contents.

Eastern Harbour. The varied menu includes seafood, grills, soups, and salads.
Tariq el Gheish el Kashafa el Baharia Club.
Tel: (203) 4805114.

Speciality Restaurants
Chez Gaby au Ritrovo ★★
Popular restaurant serving good pizzas and pasta.
22 Sharia el Hurriya.
Tel: (203) 4834404.

China House ★★
One of Alexandria's Chinese-only restaurants
Zaharan Mall, Semoaha.
Tel: (203) 4242444.

El Farida Restaurant ★★
Also located in the El-Salamlek Palace Hotel, El Farida specialises in Italian food, although international cuisine is also available.
Montazah Palace Gardens, Montazah.
Tel: (203) 5477999.

Sea Gull ★★
Built like a castle, dedicated to seafood.
Sharia Agami, Mex.
Tel: (203) 4455575.

Middle Eastern
El Ekhlaas ★★
Very good oriental cuisine.
49 Sharia Safiya Zaghloul.

Fuul Mohammed Ahmed ★
The best place for cheap, simple Egyptian specialities.
317 Sharia Shaker.

Café-Restaurants
Athineos ★
Café, patisserie, and light meals served at this one-time Greek place, ornate though overly refurbished.
21 Midan Sa'ad Zaghlul.
Tel: (203) 4820421.

Pastroudis ★★
Founded in 1923, this, along with the Cecil Hotel, is the Alexandrian institution most mentioned in Lawrence Durrell's *Alexandria Quartet.* Restaurant,

Pastroudis – one of Alexandria's institutions

patisserie, and indoor/outdoor café.
39 Sharia el Hurriya.
Tel: (203) 4929609.

Trianon ★★
Indoor café, patisserie, and restaurant; Art Nouveau decor. This was a favourite haunt of the poet Cavafy, whose office was in the building above.
Midan Sa'ad Zaghlul.
Tel: (203) 4820986.

CAIRO
Western-Style Food
Le Chalet and Le Château ★/★★
Twin restaurants owned by Swissair with coffee-shop snacks downstairs, and chic dining upstairs.
Nasr Building, Sharia el Nil, Giza.
Tel: (202) 7486270.

La Chesa ★★
Operated by Swissair Restaurants, this is a haven of Swiss cleanliness, excellent food, and a fine cake and pastry section.
21 Sharia Adli, downtown.
Tel: (202) 3939360.

Estoril ★
French food in plain surroundings but served by elaborately costumed Nubians.
12 Sharia Talaat Harb, downtown.
Tel: (202) 5743102.

Treat yourself to a *shwarma*

Justine ★★★
Reputed to be one of the best and certainly the most expensive restaurant in Cairo, the cuisine is nouvelle, and the atmosphere formal.
4 Sharia Hassan Sabri, Zamalek.
Tel: (202) 7362961.

Khan al-Khalili ★★
In the heart of the bazaar, this restaurant serves European and Egyptian food. Good for snacks, and has the cleanest toilets in the area.
5 Sikkat el Badistan, Khan el Khalili.
Tel: (202) 5903788.

Speciality Restaurants
Il Piccolo Mondo ★★
A pleasant, bustling Italian restaurant on board Le Pacha boat, moored in Zamalek.
Le Pacha Boat, Saraya el Gezira, Zamalek.
Tel: (202) 7356730.

Kandahar ★★
Indian food eaten to the accompaniment of Indian music.
3 Gammat El Dowal St, Mohandessin.
Tel: (202) 3030615.

American Fish Market ★★
Choose your own fish on this popular boat moored on the Nile.
26 Nile Street, Agonza.
Tel: (202) 5709693.

Papillon ★★★
Good Lebanese food in elegant surroundings.
Opp. Tirana Club, 26 July St, Mohandessin.
Tel: (202) 3471672.

Greek Club ★
Simple food and cheap beer are served in this pleasant restaurant overlooking the square. Roof terrace.
21 Sharia Bassiouni (first floor), downtown.
Tel: (202) 5750822.

The Nile Pharaoh ★★★
A cruising restaurant which looks like a pharaonic sailing barge. Operated by the Oberoi Hotels group, owners of the Mena House. There are both lunch and dinner cruises.
For reservations and boarding directions, tel: (202) 726122.

Middle Eastern Restaurants
Alfi Bey ★
Traditional Egyptian and Levantine food is served in old-style surroundings. No alcohol is served.

Eating in style in an expensive restaurant

3 Sharia el Alfy, downtown. Tel: (202) 771888.

Arabesque ★★

This is an elegant restaurant with a small friendly bar; adjoining it is a small gallery of works by Egyptian artists. The cuisine is Egyptian, Lebanese, and Continental. Prices are moderate, but drinking imported wine will make it expensive.

6 Sharia Qasr el Nil, downtown.
Tel: (202) 5747898.

Casino des Pigeons ★★

Pigeon and chicken, grilled or stuffed, with good hors d'oeuvres and salads. The dining is outdoors among palms and papyrus.

155 Bahr el Azam, near the Gîza Bridge, Gîza.
Tel: (202) 5721299.

Felfela ★

Though popular with tourists and foreign residents, it is also a favourite with Egyptians, and the food is certainly good. Tree trunks serve as tables. The speciality is *fool* in all its varied preparations, but the menu extends to meat dishes, ice creams, etc.

15 Sharia Hoda Sharawi, just off Sharia Talaat Harb. Tel: (202) 3922751.

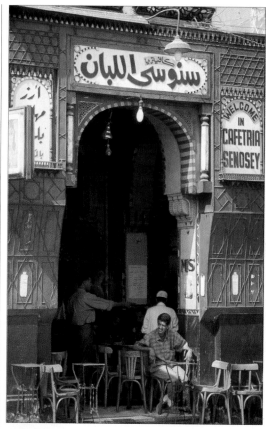

Take time out to have a cup of tea, especially with mint

Odeon Palace Hotel Restaurant ★

A 24-hour restaurant and bar appealing to journalists, actors, artists, and tourists. The food is Egyptian.

6 Sharia Abd el Hamid Shahad, off Sharia Talaat Harb, downtown.
Tel: (202) 5767971.

Cafés

Fishawi's, Cairo's oldest teahouse, is one café you should not miss for its atmosphere of old Cairo. It is in a small alley running parallel to the west side of the square in front of the Sayyidna el Hussein Mosque in Khan el Khalili.

Accommodation

The number of hotels in Egypt has increased tremendously over the past 10 years, although most are still in established centres and at the upper end of the market. The most rapid development has been at the Red Sea resorts and in Sinai. Middle category accommodation has also increased somewhat, especially in Cairo. This has taken off some of the pressure, but it is still a good idea to make advance reservations – in Upper Egypt, the Red Sea, and Sinai during the winter, in Alexandria, during the summer, or if you have your heart set on a particular hotel, anywhere, at any time.

CRUISE BOOKING

A number of boats of all categories are privately owned by hotels and other companies in Egypt, and keep changing all the time. For information regarding Nile or Lake Nasser cruises contact Thomas Cook in Egypt, your nearest travel agent, or use the internet.

Reservations are best made through Thomas Cook or another good travel agent. The international chain hotels can be booked by contacting one of their hotels or reservation centres in your own country. You may be asked to deposit a credit card.

Bear in mind that some areas of the country, such as the Delta, and along the Nile, apart from Minya, Luxor, and Aswân, will only rarely have any decent hotels. In these areas, plan your tour in terms of centres from which you can make day excursions. A Nile cruise (*see pp162–3*) is another way of getting round the problem. It is usually less expensive to buy an all-inclusive package than to make your own arrangements.

Star Rating
Hotels in Egypt are officially rated from 5-star (luxury) to 1-star. The rating system is not always evenly graduated, however, and you may find that a 3-star

hotel is just as good as a 4-star one, or that two 4-star hotels, even in the same place, vary in quality and charge markedly different rates. As a rule of thumb, any hotel

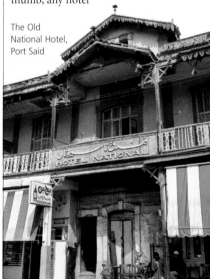

The Old National Hotel, Port Said

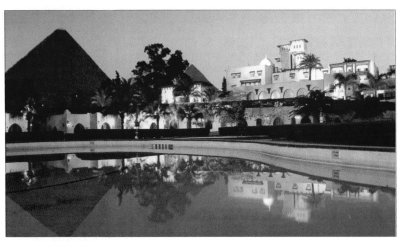
Mena House Oberoi hotel overlooking the dramatic site of the Pyramids

from three stars upwards will be acceptable; below that you should inspect the place and your room before committing yourself.

There are also hotels that have no star ratings, and also youth hostels. By and large these should be given a wide berth, though you will occasionally learn through word of mouth of some place that is acceptable.

The Bill

In addition to the basic charge for a room, service charges and tax together amount to between 15–20 per cent. Breakfast is often an obligatory extra. Single rooms or single occupancy of a double room costs 10 to 20 per cent less than the doubles rate. Rates in Cairo are often higher than elsewhere, and remain roughly the same year-round. In Alexandria they are about 10 per cent lower in winter; in Upper Egypt, the Red Sea, and Sinai they are about 10 per cent

lower in summer. Other factors affecting rates include the view and, in the lower categories, bath facilities in the room.

Hotels quote room rates both in US dollars and Egyptian pounds. Here they are given in dollars.

Double room rates in Cairo
5-star: $150–$200+
4-star: $100–$150
3-star: $65–$100
2-star: $25–$65
1-star: up to $25

Double room rates elsewhere
5-star: $100–$150+
4-star: $50–$100
3-star: $30–$50
2-star: $15–$30
1-star: up to $15

At Coptic monasteries there is no charge, though a donation would not go amiss. Accommodation is clean and basic. For further details on staying at Coptic monasteries, see *pp178–9*.

Egypt's Legendary Hotels

In the pre-air-conditioned age of grand tourism, from the late 19th century to the mid-20th century, Egypt boasted a number of gloriously cavernous hotels where sunlight filtered through louvred doors and mosquito nets wavered in the evening breezes. Garden sounds and fragrances crept into the rooms, along with the occasional beetle and drift of sand. There was an atmosphere of worn elegance, though when the plaster began falling off the walls, and the doors off their hinges, not even another gin was sufficient to restore the ambience for some tastes.

Too many of these wonderful old places were torn down and replaced by nondescript hotels. Some, however, have been restored and modernised without too much violence being done to their character.

CAIRO

With the Pyramids on its doorstep, the **Mena House Oberoi** enjoys one of the world's most spectacular locations. It began life as a khedival hunting lodge, becoming a hotel in 1869. This is now the old wing, magnificently decorated, where you can sit on the terrace of your suite with beautiful gardens below, and exchange stares with 5,000 years of history. It was here that Churchill and Roosevelt met during World War II to initiate plans for the Allies' D-Day invasion of Normandy.

The **Cairo Marriott Hotel**, or 'The Palace', was built by the Khedive Ismail Ali in honour of the Empress Eugenie of France and her husband, who had been invited to attend the festivities for the opening of the Suez Canal in 1869. The central part of the hotel still retains its character, artefacts, and decoration from that time, despite its modern use.

Early this century, Baedeker ranked Cairo's miraculously still standing 3-star **Windsor Hotel** just below the old Shepheard's, since when it has not changed a bit. Its character is literally peeling off its walls, just as its mattresses sag heavily with the weight of history. Even if you do not stay here, you should visit its delightful bar-cum-

CAIRO

Mena House Oberoi

Sharia al-Ahram, Gîza.

Tel: (202) 3833222;
www.oberoihotels.com

Marriott Hotel,

Saraya el Gezira, Zamalek.

Tel: (202) 7358888; email:
marriott@hotmail.com

Windsor Hotel,

19 Sharia Alfi Bey.

Tel: (202) 5915277.

ALEXANDRIA

Cecil Hotel

Midan Sa'ad Zaghoul.

Tel: (203) 4834856;
e-mail: h1726@accor-
hotels.com

LUXOR

Old Winter Palace

Sharia el Nil.

Tel: (209) 380422.

ASWÂN

Old Cataract Hotel

Sharia Abtal el Tahrir.

Tel: (209) 316000; email:
1666@accor-hotels.com

lounge-cum-dining room, hung with weird curios and damaged paintings, where beers are served by berobed waiters.

ALEXANDRIA

If you stay at the **Cecil Hotel**, make sure you have a room commanding the magnificent view over the Eastern Harbour, where the Mediterranean splashes against the Corniche. You will see the site of the Pharos on the breakwater in the distance, and off to the right on the Silsileh headland you can imagine the palace of the Ptolemies. If that is not enough, what other hotel can say that Cleopatra put the asp to her breast just outside their front door? A Moorish pile built in 1930, the Cecil figures often in Lawrence Durrell's *Alexandria Quartet*. Ask to see the visitors' book.

LUXOR

In Luxor, the heyday of early 20th-century leisured travel is represented by the up-market **Old Winter Palace**. At the rear, the rooms overlook the gardens, while the Nile flows by out front. King Farouk's suite was over the main entrance. Any of the other rooms overlooking the Theban necropolis and the Valley of the Kings are also good.

ASWÂN

If you saw the film of Agatha Christie's *Death on the Nile*, you will recall Aswân's **Old Cataract Hotel**, probably the loveliest place to stay in all Egypt. Built in 1902, it is a period delight over-looking the southern tip of Elephantine Island. Its highlight is the terrace, an unforgettable place to sit while the sun is setting watching *feluccas* flit like swallows in the Nile below.

View from the Cairo Tower, El Gezirah

On Business

Business Advice

Volumes could be written on matters of law, finance, and taxation as affecting business; suffice to say that visitors contemplating entering into a contract in Egypt, investing in the country, or establishing a business there, should first make enquiries in their home country with government departments, their bank, their legal advisor, and others, as appropriate, and with the Egyptian embassy there. In Egypt they should contact the commercial affairs section of their own embassy. Most countries have embassies in Cairo, and consulates in Alexandria (see p180).

Business Facilities

Most Cairo 5-star hotels have business centres which provide secretarial and translation services – usually for both guests and visitors. They will also do photocopying, send and receive faxes, etc. You can use their computer facilities and hold small meetings. Also, most 5-star hotels throughout Egypt can provide basic business facilities in guests' rooms – data lines, and sometimes small work stations. Many of the higher category hotels can at least provide you with a fax service There are also numerous internet cafés throughout Egypt, in all major cities and towns.

Additionally, the courier service, DHL, is represented in all major cities in Egypt, and can ship business documents, gifts, or holiday purchases, home. Their offices and many bazaars carry special envelopes and boxes for the purpose. Further information from their head office in Mohandessin, which is open 24 hours a day. All other branches are open 9am–5pm.
16, Lebanon St, Mohandessin. Tel: (202) 3029801.

Business Hours

Most businesses run their working day from 9am to 5pm. Government offices close on Thursdays and Fridays, and foreign embassies are closed on Fridays, the Muslim day of rest, and possibly Saturday. Businesses may be closed on Fridays or on Sundays, and additionally, on Saturdays. Expect hours of business, or the willingness to conduct business energetically, to be reduced during the month of Ramadan.

Conference and Exhibition Centres

All Cairo's big 5-star hotels offer conference and/or exhibition facilities, with the Marriott, the Semiramis Inter-Continental, and the Mena House Oberoi being the most popular. Large-scale exhibitions are generally held at the Cairo International Conference Centre, ten minutes from the airport.
Nasr Road, Nasr City. Tel: (202) 2634637.

Customs

Customs regulations permit the free import of all personal effects, whether used or new, including such items as word processors and recorders. Nor is there any restriction on the amount of money you bring into the country. Like other visitors to Egypt, a businessman bringing in electronic goods should be sure to complete customs declarations, and should hold on to a copy to present on departure, if necessary.

Etiquette

Personal relationships are an essential part of Egyptian business life and a face-to-face discussion is always preferable to the telephone. At business meetings a suit should be worn, as casual clothing is viewed as disrespectful. Business entertainment is invariably conducted at restaurants rather than at home, and generally without the involvement of spouses. Decision-making here is a slow process. Exercise patience.

Media

One initial, if somewhat thin, source of useful information is the daily English-language newspaper *The Egyptian Gazette* (on Saturdays it is called *The Egyptian Mail*). This contains a list of all ministry telephone numbers, the daily exchange rate, and gold and silver prices, as well as prayer times, and advertisements for entertainments, rentals, and business services. For greater depth there is the *Al-Ahram Weekly*, an offshoot of Egypt's distinguished daily newspaper, published every Thursday in English. Its coverage includes Egyptian and Arabic affairs, the economy and investment, culture, the environment, health care, life style, sports, fashion, entertainment, and travel. The advertisements also may prove helpful.

There are also several publications which will provide important phone numbers, contacts, and resource lists, including *Business Review*, *Insight Magazine*, the porter, and *Egypt Today*.

To keep abreast of events generally, European newspapers are usually available in Egypt the following day, and the major international current affairs magazines are widely distributed.

Radio and TV

On any radio with a medium-wave band, you can tune in to the BBC World Service, which broadcasts on 639KHz from 8.45am to noon, 3pm to 5pm, and from 7pm to 9pm; it also broadcasts on 1393KHz from 9pm to 3am. Five-star hotels pipe CNN and other television news services straight into your room.

Egyptian radio has 10-minute English-language news broadcasts on 95FM at 7.30am, 2.30pm, and 8pm, while Egyptian television's Second Channel presents an English-language news programme at 8pm.

Visas

If you are not actually running a business within the country but are simply making a business trip, there is no reason why you should not simply state 'tourism' as your reason for visiting, in which case the visa details as described in the **Practical Guide** section will apply (*see p176*).

Business Hours

Government offices: 9am–2pm, except Thu & Fri; 10am–1pm, during Ramadan. Private sector offices: 8.30am–5pm, except Fri & Sat.

Practical Guide

Arriving
Entry Formalities
Almost all visitors to Egypt require a visa and a passport still valid for at least six months. Tourist visas can be obtained in person (usually in 24 hours) or by post (allow between four and eight weeks) from an Egyptian consulate abroad, preferably in your own country. You can also obtain a visa on arrival at Cairo, Luxor, Sharm el Sheikh, and Hurghada airports, and at the port of Alexandria. Single-entry and multiple-entry (three-visit) visas each permit you to stay a maximum of one month within three months of application. You can extend your visa for a month while in Egypt. The cost of a visa will depend on your nationality and the place of application. Hotels will take a photocopy of your passport for registration purposes. On escorted tours registration is normally seen to by the tour manager.

By Air
International flights arrive into Luxor, Sharm el Sheikh, and Hurghada, apart from Cairo. If flying EgyptAir into Cairo, you arrive at Terminal 1; all other airlines arrive at Terminal 2. Immigration procedure is straight-forward, but queues can be long. If you do not already have a visa, go to one of the banks near the immigration barrier and purchase a visa stamp. Present it together with your passport and landing card to the immigration officer. Customs inspection is usually cursory for tourists. Cairo airport has duty-free shops in the arrival and departure lounges. See **Customs Regulations** (*p179*). You should remember to confirm your flight 72 hours before departure. *For flight information: tel: (202) 2914255/66/77.*

To and from the Airport
It is possible to get a public bus (No. 356 from Terminals 1 and 2; and minibus No. 27 from Terminal 1). These take one hour between Cairo Airport (Matar el Qahira) and Midan el Tahrir in central Cairo. It is almost infinitely preferable, however, for reasons of convenience, comfort, and speed, to take a limousine or a taxi.

The journey time is about half an hour. Limousines (usually large Volvos, Mercedes, and Peugeots) form a rank right outside the door and will charge at least LE45 into Cairo, more towards the Pyramids. Cheaper taxis (usually beat-up smaller cars) lurk beyond; the important thing is to agree to a price in advance. Returning to the airport also involves bargaining, but the price will usually be lower.

There is also a fast, comfortable, and reasonably priced bus service from the airport to Alexandria. The journey takes about 3½ hours. Enquire at the SuperJet bus counter within the arrivals hall.

By Sea
There are no longer any regular ferry services to Egypt from Italy and Greece. Daily ferries run between Aqaba in Jordan and Nuweiba in Sinai.

By Land

Bureaucracy prevents most people from entering by car, but a vehicle can be brought into Egypt for three months if you have an *international triptyque* or a *carnet de passage de douane* issued by the automobile club of the country where the car is registered.

Camping

The few organised campsites in Egypt are mostly along the coasts and, more often than not, are without shade or adequate facilities. Some hotels provide prepared tents and camp beds. Camping on beaches can get you in trouble if you do not check with the local police first; it can also be dangerous, as some beaches are mined. Desert camping is generally less of a problem, but you should still make enquiries and attempt to obtain permission first; any land which is near water almost certainly belongs to someone.

Children

Children are more susceptible than adults to changes in diet, to dehydration, extremes of temperature, and exposure to sun, and so extra care should be taken. For general medical advice, consult your doctor well before departure. Take sun block with you – it is expensive in Egypt.

Egyptians are generally very fond of children, but have a robust attitude towards them – as though they are expected not to fall down excavation pits or get run over by traffic. Do not assume that the same safety measures apply in Egypt as at home; far from it. Small children who do not need an entire seat to themselves, can travel free on buses and trains. Children under two years of age travel free on planes, and up to the age of 12 pay half fare. *(See Children pp156–7.)*

Climate

Average temperatures in Egypt can seem surprisingly low. Cairo averages 14°C in January, 30°C in August, but these figures mask considerable extremes between night and daytime temperatures which are the result of the surrounding desert.

The coastal positions of Alexandria on the Mediterranean and, to a lesser extent, Hurghada on the Red Sea, reduce these extremes, and also give them a more even year-round temperature. As you move southwards, the air becomes drier and average temperatures increase.

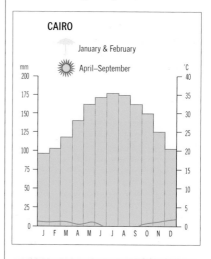

Weather Conversion Chart
25.4mm = 1 inch
°F = 1.8 x °C + 32

ALEXANDRIA

November–February

May–September

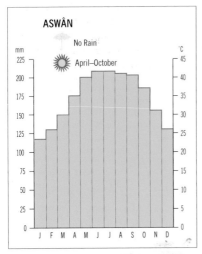

ASWÂN

No Rain

April–October

Clothing

In winter you will need some woollens; in summer, light cottons. In spring and autumn a combination of both is advisable against warm days and cool nights. In summer, at least one sweater is handy, as the deserts can be really cool as soon as the sun goes down.

Alexandria has strong sea breezes. Take warm clothes if planning to sleep outdoors in winter (such as on a *felucca*). Clothes should be light in colour to reflect the sun and be easily washable and drip-dry. Bring comfortable walking shoes. Allow for conservative standards of dress. Wear trousers rather than shorts, skirts which fall to the knee, shirts and blouses which cover the shoulders and upper arms.

Conversion Tables
See box, opposite page.

Coptic Monasteries
Permission is not required to visit most monasteries in Egypt (*see pp66–7*). All are open to both men and women, but neither sex should wear revealing clothes. The following information applies to all Coptic monasteries.

The monasteries do not have set hours for visiting, but bearing in mind the monks' dawn and evening prayers, it is best to visit between 9am and 4pm.

The Coptic Church goes in for a great deal of fasting, and a monastery may forbid entry to all or part of its enclosure during these days. To confirm details of openings you should enquire first at the Coptic Patriarchate, Cathedral of St Mark, 222 Sharia Ramses, Abbassia, Cairo (*tel: (202) 4831822*). It would be a good idea to check here too if you wish to stay overnight at a monastery, though there is a good chance of your being allowed to if you simply show up.

The Greek Orthodox St Catherine's Monastery is closed on Fridays and Sundays, but is otherwise open to

Conversion Table		
FROM	TO	MULTIPLY BY
Inches	Centimetres	2.54
Feet	Metres	0.3048
Yards	Metres	0.9144
Miles	Kilometres	1.6090
Acres	Hectares	0.4047
Gallons	Litres	4.5460
Ounces	Grams	28.35
Pounds	Grams	453.6
Pounds	Kilograms	0.4536
Tons	Tonnes	1.0160

To convert back, for example from centimetres to inches, divide by the number in the third column.

Men's Suits

UK	36	38	40	42	44	46	48
Rest of Europe	46	48	50	52	54	56	58
US	36	38	40	42	44	46	48

Dress Sizes

UK	8	10	12	14	16	18
France	36	38	40	42	44	46
Italy	38	40	42	44	46	48
Rest of Europe	34	36	38	40	42	44
US	6	8	10	12	14	16

Men's Shirts

UK	14	14.5	15	15.5	16	16.5	17
Rest of Europe	36	37	38	39/40	41	42	43
US	14	14.5	15	15.5	16	16.5	17

Men's Shoes

UK	7	7.5	8.5	9.5	10.5	11
Rest of Europe	41	42	43	44	45	46
US	8	8.5	9.5	10.5	11.5	12

Women's Shoes

UK	4.5	5	5.5	6	6.5	7
Rest of Europe	38	38	39	39	40	41
US	6	6.5	7	7.5	8	8.5

visitors from 9am to noon. Staying overnight is not permitted.

Crime
You and your possessions are generally safe in Egypt. Nevertheless, take special care with passports, tickets, and money. Hotels will look after your valuables for you, but you should obtain a receipt.

Customs Regulations
All personal effects are exempt from duty. If you are asked to list these on a customs declaration form, make sure you leave with what you brought in, or you may be charged duty. If you lose anything, report it to the police and get them to give you written confirmation (you will also need this for insurance). You are also free to bring in any amount of foreign currency. Video cameras must be declared and registered in passports. On departure, the stamp in your passport will be cancelled.

You are permitted to bring in one litre of alcohol, plus 200 cigarettes or 250g of tobacco or 25 cigars free of duty. There are duty-free shops at Cairo Airport both before and after customs.

The export of antiquities or any item over 100 years old without a licence is strictly forbidden.

Driving
To hire a car you must have a driving licence and be between 25 and 70 years of age. Car hire is not expensive, and petrol is cheap. You can make arrangements with one of the major international companies from abroad, or choose from these and local

companies when in Egypt. Hertz and Budget have desks at Cairo Airport and offices in Cairo, and most major hotels in Cairo and Alexandria will have agency desks.

Third-party insurance is compulsory (make sure that it is included). Check that everything essential actually works (like brakes), that you have been given a spare tyre and other necessary equipment, and make a note beforehand of any dents or damage.

There are plenty of petrol stations in the cities, but they can be few and far between on the open road, so always try to keep your tank topped up.

Your main problem will be other traffic. Cairo is a madhouse on wheels, while country roads are busy with trucks, donkeys, and camels. Traffic drives on the right, although you would not immediately guess it; the practice is to meander, go down one-way streets the wrong way, jump lights, and so on. Avoid driving at night: vehicles do not always bother to use their lights, many have none, or beam whatever they do have into your face.

Hiring a car with a driver will not cost much more than self-drive. Or, you should consider hiring a taxi for the half-day or day, agreeing on the destinations and price beforehand.

Drugs

Do not bring drugs into the country or use any while there. Possession is a serious offence, while smuggling and dealing involves mandatory sentences of either life imprisonment or death. If carrying prescribed drugs, get a doctor's letter, just in case you are stopped.

Electricity

Electrical current is 220 volts AC. Sockets take the standard continental European round two-pronged plug.

Embassies and Consulates

The following is an abbreviated list of embassies and consulates in Cairo. A complete list can be found in the *Cairo A–Z* and *Cairo: A Practical Guide*, two widely available local publications.

Some countries also maintain consulates in both Alexandria and in Port Said.

Australia Cairo Plaza Tower, 1097 Corniche el Nil, Boulaq. *Tel: (202) 777900.*

Canada 5 El Saraya Kobra Square, Garden City. *Tel: (202) 7943110.*

Ireland 3 Abu el Feda Tower, north of the Zamalek Bridge, Zamalek. *Tel: (202) 7358264.*

New Zealand Consular affairs are handled by the UK.

UK 7 Sharia Ahmed Raghab, Garden City. *Tel: (202) 7940850.*

US 5 Sharia America Latina, Garden City. *Tel: (202) 7957371.*

Egyptian Embassies Abroad

Australia 1 Darwin Avenue, Yarralumla, Canberra. *Tel: (06) 7234437.*

Canada 454 Laurier Avenue East, Ottawa, Ontario K1P 5P4. *Tel: (613) 234 4931.*

UK 75 South Audley Street, London. *Tel: (0207) 499 2401.*

US 2300 Decatur Plaza NW, Washington DC 20008. *Tel: (202) 234 3903.*

Emergency Telephone Numbers

The following are Cairo numbers.

Emergency (general): *123*
Ambulance: *(202) 5770123*
Fire brigade: *125*
Police: *122*
Tourist police (general): *126*
Tourist police: *(202) 3655556* (Cairo Airport), *(202) 3959116* (downtown), *(202) 3850259* (the Pyramids).

Thomas Cook Emergency Assistance

Report within 24 hours the loss or theft of Thomas Cook travellers' cheques, using their 24-hour reverse charges telephone number: *00 44 1733 318950* (reverse charges).

Emergency assistance can also be obtained from the local offices of Thomas Cook listed on page 186.

Glossary

Abu: holy man or saint, whether Muslim or Christian.
Ankh: the hieroglyphic sign for life.
Bab: gate.
Bayt: house.
Cartouche: in hieroglyphics, the oval band enclosing the god's or pharaoh's name and symbolising continuity.
Copt: a Christian of the native Egyptian Church.
Corniche: seafront or riverfront road.
Deir: monastery.
Fellahin: Egyptian peasants; the singular is *fellah.*
Harem: the private family (or the women's) quarter in a house.
Hypostyle: a hypostyle hall is any chamber whose ceiling is supported by columns or pillars.
Iconostasis: in a church, the alter screen to which icons are attached.

Ka: in ancient Egypt, the spirit believed to inhabit the body during life.
Khan: an inn built around a courtyard for travelling merchants and their animals. Also called an *okel* or *wakala.*
Khedive: viceroy (Mohammed Ali and his descendants ruled Egypt as the nominal viceroys of the Ottoman sultan until World War I, whereafter they ruled as kings).
Madrasa: a mosque serving as a theological school.
Mashrabiyya: wooden screenwork, often used in windows.
Mausoleum: domed tomb chamber.
Midan: a square.
Mihrab: a mosque's wall niche indicating the direction of Mecca.
Minbar: the pulpit in a mosque.
Moulid: anniversary celebration of a Muslim or Christian holy person.
Muezzin: the person who makes the call to prayer from a minaret.
Naos: the sanctuary of a temple.
Narthex: a church's entrance vestibule.
Pylon: monumental temple gateway.
Sharia: street.

Health

No inoculation or vaccination certificates are required for entry into Egypt unless you are arriving from an infected area. Your doctor, however, may recommend precautions against yellow fever, cholera, typhoid, hepatitis A, tetanus, and polio. Malaria is both seasonal and regional; check with your doctor before you go, and if you do need a prophylaxis, take it.

Bites of all kinds need the immediate attention of a doctor. Inflammation of the eyes can be indicative of trachoma, while contact with stagnant water can cause bilharzia; the former should be dealt with immediately, the latter can await a check-up at a tropical diseases hospital at home. Do not swim in lakes, rivers, or streams, as these are sure places for picking up water-borne diseases. Your hotel, embassy, or any pharmacist can recommend a doctor, most of whom will speak English or French.

In an emergency, the following private hospitals in Cairo are best. However, it is likely that you will need to hand over a cash payment or at least a substantial deposit in advance.

Al Salam Hospital

Syria St, Mohandessin.
Tel: (202) 3029091/2/3.

As Salam International Hospital

Corniche el Nil, Maadi.
Tel: (202) 5240250/5240077.

You may well suffer a brief upset stomach, a normal reaction to a change of diet and climate which passes after a few days. Eat plain food and drink a lot, but if it lasts too long, consult a doctor. There is no need to stop eating Egyptian

Hitching a free ride

food if you feel well enough to eat at all. Your system, used to the microbes back home, will adjust to the local variety. Standard preparations for stomach upsets are available at pharmacies.

While eating in Egypt be scrupulously hygienic. Make sure your food has been properly washed and prepared. Provided even the simplest eating place has running water, there should be no problem. If in doubt, avoid salads and ice-cream and stick to hot dishes. Although drinking water is heavily chlorinated and theoretically safe, stick to bottled mineral water.

Remember that the sun can be hot at any time of year, and the temperature can fall off sharply at night. During the day you should wear a head covering and sunglasses. It is not advisable to drink spirits before sundown as this causes dehydration, nor to consume iced drinks during the heat of the day.

A high-screen suntan lotion is advisable, especially if you are in the desert. Insect repellent is very useful.

Hitch-hiking

You will be expected to pay for a ride. Lone women should not hitch-hike.

Insurance

You should take out personal travel insurance before leaving, from your travel agent, tour operator, or insurance company. It should give adequate cover for medical expenses, loss and theft, personal liability (but liability arising from motor accidents is not usually included – see below), and cancellation expenses. Always read the conditions, any exclusions, and details of cover, and check that the amount of cover is adequate.

Report any losses or thefts to the tourist police immediately, and get an officially stamped statement, without which most insurance companies will refuse to pay claims money.

If you hire a car, collision insurance, often called collision damage waiver or CDW, is normally offered by the hirer, and is usually compulsory. Check with your own motor insurers before you leave, as you may be covered by your normal policy. If not, CDW is payable locally and may be as much

as 50 per cent of the hiring fee. Neither CDW nor your personal travel insurance will protect you for liability arising out of an accident in a hire car, for example, if you damage another vehicle or injure someone. If you are likely to hire a car, you should obtain such extra cover, preferably from your travel agent or other insurer before departure.

Media

English language publications are *The Egyptian Gazette* (or *The Egyptian Mail* on Saturdays), the fortnightly *Cairo Times, Al-Ahram Weekly* (Thursdays), and the monthly magazine *Egypt Today*. There is daily television news in English at 8pm on Channel 2, and the Nile TV Channel 9 also broadcasts in English.

Money Matters

The Egyptian pound (LE) is divided into 100 piastres (PT). Notes are for 10, 25, and 50 piastres, and 1, 5, 10, 20, 50, and 100 pounds. Egyptian currency can be purchased abroad.

Banks have exchange counters at Cairo Airport and major hotels throughout Egypt. Thomas Cook, Travelex, and American Express also change money.

Major brands of travellers' cheques such as Thomas Cook, denominated in sterling or US dollars, are generally accepted at exchange counters, banks, and major hotels and shops. The Thomas Cook locations listed on page 186 will cash Thomas

Pharmacy shop sign

Cook travellers' cheques free of commission. Credit and charge cards such as MasterCard, VISA, and American Express are accepted at major hotels and shops. Always keep your receipts for exchange transactions.

Banks are generally open from 8.30am–2pm Sunday to Thursday. If you need to transfer money quickly, use the MoneyGram℠ Money to Egypt Transfer service, available through all Thomas Cook locations listed on the next page. Take some identification with you and you will be able to receive money in minutes from over 100 countries. For more details, go to your nearest Thomas Cook location, or call Freephone 0800 897198 (UK).

LANGUAGE

The language of Egypt is Arabic. Its alphabet differs from that of Western languages, making phonetic transliteration difficult. English is taught to every school child, so you will probably find yourself widely understood. Nevertheless, here are some helpful basics.

BASICS

Yes	aywa or nam
No	la
Please	minfadlak
	(if addressing a man)
	minfadlik
	(if addressing a woman)
Thank you	shukran
No thank you	la shukran
Good	kuwayyis
Bad	mish kuwayyis
God willing	inshallah

GREETINGS

Welcome	ahlan wa sahlan
(response)	ahlan bik
Hello (formal)	assalaamu aleikum
(response)	wa aleikum assalaam
Hello (informal)	saeeda
Hello/goodbye (informal)	sabah el kheir
Goodbye	ma salaama

CALENDAR

Today	innaharda
Tomorrow	bukra
Yesterday	imbarrih
Day	youm
Week	usbua
Month	shahr
Year	sana
Sunday	youm il ahad
Monday	youm il itnayn
Tuesday	youm it talaat
Wednesday	youm il arbah
Thursday	youm il khamees
Friday	youm il gumah
Saturday	youm is sabt

NUMBERS

0	sifr	13	talatarsha
1	wahad	14	arbahtarsha
2	itnayn	15	khamastarsha
3	talaata	16	sittarsha
4	arbah	17	sabahtarsha
5	khamsa	18	tamantarsha
6	sitta	19	tisahtarsha
7	sabah	20	ahshreen
8	tamanya	21	wahad waahshreen
9	tesah	30	talaateen
10	ahshara	100	miyya
11	hidarsha	500	khamsa miyya
12	itnarsha	1000	alf

National Holidays

Banks and offices will be closed on:

1 January New Year's Day
25 April Liberation Day
1 May Labour Day
23 July Revolution Day
6 October Forces Day
23 October Suez Day
23 December Victory Day

There are also many religious holidays, both Islamic and Christian. The Islamic calendar is lunar-based, and because its year is usually 11 days shorter than the solar Western calendar, Islamic holidays occur about 11 days earlier each successive year.

The most important of these holidays is Ramadan, the month of fasting,

DIRECTIONS	
Where is Hotel ...?	feyn funduk il ...?
Where is the bank?	feyn il bank?
Where is the bus station?	feyn mahattat il autobees?
Where is the train station?	feyn mahattat il atr?
Where is the airport?	feyn il mataar?
Where is the restaurant?	feyn il matam?
Where is the toilet?	feyn il twalet?
Left/right/straight ahead	shimaal/yimeen/alatool

REQUESTS & SHOPPING	
There is/is there?	fi/fi?
I (do not) want	(mish) aayiz (if you are male); (mish) ayza (if you are female)
How much?	bekaam?
It is too expensive	da ghaali awi
Bigger/smaller	akbar/asghar

REMARKS	
I do not understand	ana mish fahem (if you are male); ana mish fahma (if you are female)
I am tired/unwell	ana taaban (if you are male); ana taabana (if you are female)
I am (not) married	ana (mish) mitgawwiz (if you are male); ana (mish) mitgawwisa (if you are female)
Go away	imshee
Never mind	maalesh
Impossible	mish mumkin
Leave me	sebne
Excuse me	laow samat

during which working hours are often shortened, and effort is generally curtailed.

Opening Hours

Generally, department stores and shops are open from 9am to 1pm and from 5pm to 8pm or later (9am to 7pm in winter), though in areas heavily frequented by tourists some shops may remain open throughout the day. Some shops close on Fridays, most on Sundays.

During the month of Ramadan, shop hours are likely to be from 10.30am to 3.30pm and 8pm to 10pm or even later. (*For banks, see* Money Matters, *pp183–4.*)

Organised Tours

Tour operators around the world offer a wide choice of package tours and cruises to Egypt, ranging from one week to one month, and including all transport, accommodation, and sightseeing. **Thomas Cook, Abercrombie and Kent, Kuoni, Hayes & Jarvis,** and **Swan Hellenic** are among the leading names in tours and cruises (*see p162*).

Also very helpful is the Egyptian state agency **Misr Travel**, with offices in London, New York, and Sydney. Their head office in **Cairo** is at 1 Sharia Talaat Harb, PO Box 1000. *Tel: (202) 3930010.*
Australia Level 5, 630 George St, Sydney, NSW 2000. *Tel: (612) 9267 6979.*
UK Rooms 201–4, Langham House, 308 Regent St, London W1R 5AL. *Tel: (020) 7255 1087.*
US Suite 555, 630 5th Ave, New York, NY 10111. *Tel: (212) 582 921011.*

Thomas Cook Offices in Egypt

Alexandria 15 Midan Sa'ad Zaghloul. *Tel: (203) 4827830.*
Aswân 59 Abtal el Tahrir St, Corniche el Nil. *Tel: (209) 7324011.*
Cairo 17 Mahmoud Bassiuony St. *Tel: (202) 5747183*; World Trade Centre, 1191 Corniche el Nil St, Boulac. *Tel: (202) 5780808/9.* Thomas Cook also has branches in Dokki, Heliopolis, Maadi, and in the Semiramis Inter-Continental Hotel (*tel: (202) 3558544*).
Hurghada 8 El Sheraton St. *Tel: (2065) 443500/443338.*
Luxor Winter Palace Hotel, Corniche el Nil. *Tel: (2095) 3722196.*
Port Said 43 Goumhoria St. *Tel: (2066) 227559.*
Sharm el Sheikh Gafy Mall, Gafy Land. *Tel: (2062) 600210, ext 301.*

Pharmacies

Pharmacies in Egypt carry a full range of medicines, including many foreign brand names. They also often provide medicines available abroad only on prescription. Pharmacists are highly trained and can make helpful recommendations as to what to take. They can also refer you to well-qualified English-speaking doctors.

Photography

International brands of film are

available in all tourist areas of Egypt. While the range in print film is good, the range in transparency film is limited. Always check the 'process by' date on the film package. The sky and sands are bright, and much light reflects off the sea and the Nile, so slow film speeds of 64 ISO to 100 ISO will be fine for outdoor purposes. In museums and tombs, however, where light levels are kept low and flash photography is forbidden, you will need at least 400 ISO film. Usually the fastest film available is 200 ISO, though 400 ISO can often be found with some searching. Processing labs are plentiful in Cairo, Hurghada, Luxor, and Alexandria. Do not photograph airports, bridges, docks, railway stations, government buildings, or anything else of a potentially security sensitive nature. At the very least, you may find your film confiscated.

Places of Worship

There are Protestant, Catholic, Greek Orthodox, and Coptic churches, and also Jewish synagogues in Cairo and Alexandria. Places of worship in Cairo: **All Saints' Cathedral** (Anglican and Episcopalian) at Sharia el Gezirah, Zamalek. *Tel: (202) 7368391.* **Church of the Holy Family** (Catholic), 55 Sharia 15, Maadi. *Tel: (202) 3582004.* **Jewish Synagogue** Sharia Adli, downtown.

Police

See Emergency Telephone Numbers, *pp180–81,* and Security, *p30.*

Post Offices

The post between Egypt and abroad can be very efficient provided you use a letter box at a major hotel or in a central location, or you go to a post office. Some letter boxes, it would seem, are visited by postal employees only very rarely, if at all. Also, anything that is not a simple letter or postcard can take a very long time to arrive. In Cairo, the Central Post Office is at Midan el Ataba, near the Ezbekieh Gardens, and is open 24 hours daily. Other post offices are open 8.30am to 3pm daily, except Fridays. Most hotels can provide you with stamps for letters and postcards.

Public Transport
Air

EgyptAir, the state airline, operates frequent daily flights between Cairo and the main tourist destinations of Luxor, Aswân, Abu Simbel, Sharm el Sheikh, and Hurghada. With less frequency it serves Alexandria, Matrouh, St Catherine's, El Kharga Oasis, and the New Valley, to name but a few other places. A private airline operates from Cairo, to and from El Gouna, and there are several small charter companies operating within the country.

Always try to make reservations, especially to Upper Egypt and St Catherine's, as far in advance as possible.

Bus

Long distance buses can be fast, cheap, and comfortable. Bookings must be made in person at the relevant terminals, which in Cairo are: **To Alexandria** and **Matrouh:** SuperJet service from Cairo Airport; El Mazha – Abu Bakr St, opposite EgyptAir Hospital in Heliopolis; Abdel Moneim Riad St

near the Ramses Hilton and Midan Giza
– Morad St, by Misr Petrol Station near
the Cairo Sheraton.

To Hurghada and **Sharm El Sheikh:**
SuperJet service from El Torgoman,
behind *Al-Ahram* newspaper building
and El Mazha – address as above.

To Port Said: Superjet service from 194
Ramses Street, near the train station.

**To Ismailia, Suez, Hurghada, Sharm,
Dahab, Nuweiba, Taba, Ras Sidr,
St Catherine's, El Arish,** and **Rafah:** East
Delta bus service from El Mazha –
address as above, El Kolaly – El Galaa St,
Ramses; El Torgoman – behind *Al-
Ahram* newspaper building.

To Sharm and **Suez only:** East Delta bus
service from Crossroads of Abbassiya
and Salah Salem Roads.

To Luxor, Aswân, and **Oases:** Wageh Ibly
Bus Company: No designated stops
(*tel: (202) 2609298/2612233 for pick-up
information*). SuperJet: El MazAa (*tel:
(202) 29090170*); El Torgoman (*tel: (202)
5798181*); A Moneim Riad (*tel: (202)
5751313*); Midan Giza (*tel: (202)
5725032*); East Delta (*tel: (202) 4198533*).

Rail

Ramses Station (Mahattat Ramses),
Midan Ramses, is Cairo's main train
station. From here there are comfortable
first- and second-class trains north into
the Delta and Alexandria, and south
into Upper Egypt, and overnight
Wagons-Lits sleepers to Upper Egypt.
The fastest trains take 2 hours to
Alexandria; 11 hours to Luxor; and 15
hours to Aswân. Be sure they are air-
conditioned.

Full timetable details are in the
Thomas Cook Overseas Timetable
(published bi-monthly, obtainable from
UK branches of Thomas Cook or by
telephoning (*01733*) *416477*).

For Upper Egypt you should book a
day in advance; for Wagons-Lits a week
in advance. All services must be booked
personally at Ramses Station
(*tel: (202) 5753555 for information*).

Local Transport

City buses in Cairo and also trams in
Alexandria are generally to be avoided as
they are almost always jammed solid.

However, Cairo has a very clean,
efficient, and easy-to-use metro system.
Taxis are inexpensive. Rarely will one
operate on a meter, and drivers will
usually ask for LE10 from a foreigner for
almost any journey in Cairo or
Alexandria. In fact, LE5 will be sufficient
in all cases. Carriages are a pleasant
alternative, especially in Luxor, but they
tend to cost more than taxis.

Student and Youth Travel

Museums and sites usually offer a 50 per
cent discount to students. Some
discount is available on travel though it
is limited. Generally avoid youth hostels.

Telephones

Local and international telephone
services are available in most hotels.
Local calls can also be made from some
kiosks, shops, and restaurants.
International calls can be made from
PTT offices. In Cairo there is a 24-hour
PTT office in Midan el Tahrir. Normally
you pay first for a fixed number of
minutes. For assistance, dial *10*.
International dialling codes include:
Australia: *61*   **Canada:** *1*

Ireland: *353*   New Zealand: *64*
UK: *44*   USA: *1*

Thomas Cook

See page 186 for details of Thomas Cook offices in Egypt. Thomas Cook's website at *www.thomascook.com* provides up-to-the-minute details of Thomas Cook's services.

Time

Egypt is two hours ahead of Greenwich Mean Time.

Tipping

See Baksheesh, *p25*.

Toilets

Apart from the better hotels and restaurants, toilets can be off-putting. Never count on there being toilet paper. Squirters are sometimes provided, or a bucket of water with which you are expected to splash yourself.

Tourist Offices in Egypt

Cairo: There are Tourist Information Offices at Cairo International Airport *(tel: (202) 2454400)*, at the downtown head office, 5 Sharia Adli *(tel: (202) 3913454)*, and at the Pyramids *(tel: (202) 3838823)*. They can provide brochures, maps, and other relevant information.
Alexandria: The Tourist Information Office is in Midan Sa'ad Zaghlul *(tel: (203) 4807611)*. In both Luxor and Aswân the Tourist Offices are centrally located on the corniche.

Egyptian Tourist Offices Abroad

UK: Egyptian State Tourist Office, 170 Piccadilly, London W1V 9DE.

Tel: (020) 7493 5282.
US: 630 5th Avenue, New York, NY 10111. *Tel: (212) 332 2570.*

Travellers with Disabilities

Very few concessions are made to travellers with disabilities, either at museums or sites within the country or by foreign tour operators. Thomas Cook has made a concerted effort to develop their ground handling arrangements for travellers in wheelchairs or with mobility problems, and can arrange itineraries to suit. Contact them at their Head Office (*see p186*).

Most tombs and temples are accessible to a person in a wheelchair, including the tomb of Ramses VI in the Valley of the Kings, the Citadel, the Museum, and major mosques in Cairo. Sandy sites like Saqqâra, however, could be very difficult, but not impossible.

The railway station at Qena

ACKNOWLEDGEMENTS

Thomas Cook wishes to thank the photographers, picture libraries, and other organisations for the loan of the photographs reproduced in this book, to whom copyright in the photographs belongs.

CHERYL WYNNE-EYTON 147, 152
EGYPT TOURISM AUTHORITY 36, 72, 77, 81, 113, 157, 159, 166, 168, 171
NATURE PHOTOGRAPHERS LTD (DA SMITH) 160a, 160b, 161a, 161b, 161c
M CRAME/CHRISTINE OSBORNE PICTURES/MEP 106, back cover cut-out
CHRISTINE OSBORNE PICTURES/MEP 22, 23, 61, 75, 88, 96, 116, 154a, 154b, 155a, 155b, back cover top centre
PICTURES COLOUR LIBRARY 15, 20, 27, 43, 87, 119, 128, 137, 143, 151
SPECTRUM COLOUR LIBRARY back cover top right

The remaining pictures are held in the AA PHOTO LIBRARY and were taken by RICK STRANGE, except for page 18 (a) which was taken by CHRIS COE. Rick Strange would like to thank WINGS TOURS & NILE CRUISES for their help.

FOR LABURNUM TECHNOLOGIES

Design Director Alpana Khare
Series Director Razia Grover
Editors Madhavi Singh, Rajeev Jairam,
Deepshika Singh

Photo Editor Radhika Singh
DTP Designer Neeraj Aggarwal,
Harish Aggarwal

Thanks to Cheryl Wynne-Eyton for additional research and updating work on this edition.

Travellers

Feedback Form

Please help us improve future editions by taking part in our reader survey. Every returned form will be acknowledged. To show our appreciation we will send you a voucher entitling you to £1 off your next *Travellers* guide or any other Thomas Cook guidebook ordered direct from Thomas Cook Publishing. Just take a few minutes to complete and return this form to us.

We'd also be glad to hear of your comments, updates or recommendations on places we cover or you think that we ought to cover.

1. Which *Travellers* guide did you purchase?

_____

2. Have you purchased other *Travellers* guides in the series?

   Yes ☐

   No ☐

   If Yes, please specify_____

3. Which of the following tempted you into buying your *Travellers* guide:
   (Please tick as many as appropriate)

   The price ☐

   The FREE weblinks CD ☐

   The cover ☐

   The content ☐

   Other_____

4. What do you think of :

   a) the cover design? _____

   b) the design and layout styles within the book?_____

   c) the FREE weblinks CD?_____

5. Please tell us about any features that in your opinion could be changed, improved or added in future editions of the book or CD:

   _____

   _____

Your age category: ☐ under 21 ☐ 21-30 ☐ 31-40 ☐ 41-50 ☐ 51+

Mr/Mrs/Miss/Ms/Other

Surname_____ Initials_____

Full address: (Please include postal or zip code)_____

_____

Daytime telephone number: _____

Email address: _____

☐ Please tick here if you would be willing to participate in further customer surveys.

☐ Please tick here if you would like to receive information on new titles or special offers from Thomas Cook Publishing (please note we never give your details to third party companies).

Please detach this page and send it to: **The Editor, Travellers, Thomas Cook Publishing, PO Box 227, The Thomas Cook Business Park, Peterborough PE3 8XX, United Kingdom.**

tear along the perforation

The Editor, Travellers
Thomas Cook Publishing
PO Box 227
The Thomas Cook Business Park
Peterborough, PE3 8XX
United Kingdom